Journeys in the Light Within

Meditations by
Elizabeth Anderton Fox

Journeys in the Light Within

Meditations by
Elizabeth Anderton Fox

Megalithica Books
Stafford England

Journeys in the Light Within: Meditations by Elizabeth Anderton Fox
Elizabeth Anderton Fox
© 2020 First edition

All rights reserved, including the right to reproduce this book, or portions thereof, in any form, except for personal use, including group workshops. Authorship of this material must then be credited to Elizabeth Anderton Fox.

The rights of the individual to be identified as the author of this work have been asserted by them in accordance with the Copyright, Designs and Patents Act, 1988.

Editor: Danielle Lainton
Layout: Storm Constantine/Danielle Lainton
Cover Art and Design: Danielle Lainton

ISBN: 978-1-912241-16-3
Catalogue Number: MB0208

Set Book Antiqua

A Megalithica Books Publication
An imprint of Immanion Press
http://www.immanion-press.com

Table of Contents

Introduction	7
The Hermetic Tradition	11
Consciousness	17
The Light Within	27
A Solo Opening and Closing Ritual	32
Magical Worlds	35
The Tree of Life	45
Magical Bridges	48
Demeter and Persephone	57
Being	68
The Inner Self	71
The Search	75
Inner Cleansing	79
The Seeker	86
Wisdom, Strength and Beauty	93
The Pleiades	102
The Castle on the Shore	110
The Tree	118
The Inner Temple	123
The Star	127
The Perennial Story	130
The Rhythms of Force and Form	147
A Dream	154
Thoughts for Meditation	158

For all my Brothers and Sisters who have travelled these journeys with me.

Introduction

Welcome to our journeys of exploration in the Inner Worlds, which lie hidden within our minds and consciousness. If you are new to this kind of experience a few words of explanation and advice might be helpful. If you are familiar with this kind of working, bear with us for a short time.

Find a quiet place where you won't be disturbed and a comfortable chair which allows you to sit upright. Things like special robes, incense and candles are not necessary but can be used if you like them to create an atmosphere. Similarly, it is not necessary to start with a ritual, but I have included a short one should you wish to use it.

Before meditating or using a guided inner journey, it is good practice to wash one's hands and have a drink of water. Then settle yourself in your chair and relax. Allow your breathing to become slow and rhythmical.

To use the journeys that follow in this book it is helpful to have a like-minded companion who will read the text for you or to pre-record it for yourself.

I would suggest starting a diary of your meditation thoughts and experiences. It often happens that the significance of your experiences is not immediately apparent, they tend to surface with time and often link up with previous ones. I would also include dreams, especially any you feel are particularly 'real'.

You might ask why should you take these journeys? The answer is in what you can learn through taking them. This might be in deeper understanding of spiritual truths or learning how to deal with life's problems or finding out how the inner worlds work.

These journeys are very personal to you, everyone will respond differently. What you will learn may be different from what I learned from them, treasure what they teach you.

Now let us consider some technical bits before we proceed to the journeys.

Within every human being is a spark of the Divine; this has its own consciousness which is largely masked from consciousness of the material world. I will call these two types of consciousness spiritual and mundane. The majority of humans spend their entire lives focused in the material, mundane world.

There may be occasional flashes from spiritual consciousness, but these are seldom recognised for what they are.

It is only by deliberate effort and training that the self can become aware of the inner spiritual consciousness and the profound teachings and wisdom within it. This can be achieved by learning to control and relax the mind by the practice of meditation.

The five senses – sight, touch, smell, sound and taste – provide all information for the functioning of physical life. While these function largely automatically they can be trained to function on a more effective and deeper level.

Intuition is the sense through which contact is made with spiritual consciousness. Contact with it is very subtle, it occurs as momentary flashes of knowing. A thought, an idea or a fact just seems to rise from the depths of the mind, and it is then the function of intellectual mind to interpret and understand what has been received. Intuitional knowledge flows from the Divine source through the subconscious to surface in the conscious mind.

The question may be asked why should we wish to listen to what the voice of intuition has to say to us? It is because this is the channel through which we can access universal knowledge and wisdom.

To be able to hear the voice of intuition takes time and practice. We need to focus our attention inwardly, still the mind of its usual chatter and create an inner space where knowledge can manifest.

The techniques used by the Western Mystery Schools to access spiritual consciousness employ two main methods, symbols and visualisation.

Symbols are words or images that convey meanings which cannot adequately be expressed in language.

Visualisation is the creation of an idea in the mind so that it becomes a reality.

Individual minds function in different ways, so everyone 'visualises' in a different and personal way. For some visualisation is pictorial, and visual type images can be created in great detail. These can be seen as three-dimensional pictures which can be seen from all angles around 360 degrees. Others do not visualise in images. We can visualise – imagine – in any of the five senses. The fact that the image is not a visual one (as seen by the eye) does not reduce its effectiveness. What matters is that the image/impression is REAL to the mind within which it exists.

It is important to understand that ALL experiences are experienced within the mind, no matter whether their source is external or internal. For example, a cut may be caused by a knife, but the pain of its cut is felt by consciousness.

The inner journeys which follow are designed to open the inner self to these deep forms of knowledge and experience. The practice of meditation and visualisation allows us to have experiences every bit as vivid and as valid as those whose cause is in the physical world.

The Hermetic Tradition

The Hermetic Tradition is a magical bridge, a way by which something is brought from somewhere to somewhere. It is a means by which knowledge is transmitted from one generation to another. Such a tradition may be written, oral or symbolic in form. There may not be authentic documents from ancient times, but there are stories, traditions and fragments of past writings hidden in later ones.

Truth is eternal and shines forth from these timeless sources. It needs no sanction from previous generations, no seal of approval of authority, it speaks with its own voice within all who are prepared to listen.

The knowledge that came to be known as the Hermetic Tradition runs through our history like a thread of gold. It was known in early Byzantium and was taught in the schools that existed in Haran in South East Turkey before the Christian era. The Harranian school drew from many sources; they had their roots in Chaldea and the schools of the Magi; they harboured priceless Greek scrolls which otherwise may have been lost. Some of these scrolls were also translated into Arabic in ancient Baghdad.

This knowledge was contained in writings known as the Corpus Hermeticum, the most famous of which is The Emerald Tablet of Hermes Trismegistus. The eighteen tracts of the Corpus Hermeticum, along with the Perfect Sermon (also called the Asclepius), are the foundational documents of the Hermetic Tradition.

They were thought to have been written by an Egyptian priest or sage named Hermes or Thoth, who was given the honorific title Thrice Greatest. While they are now thought to have been written in Alexandria, Egypt in the early centuries of the Common Era, their content is thought to be a rewriting of much older material from very early teachings of the Egyptian Temples.

In the late 1400s, copies of the Hermetic documents came into the possession of Cosimo de Medici, the ruler of Florence, who immediately set Marsilio Ficino, who worked for him as a translator, to translate the documents into Latin. Ficino translated the first fourteen treatises of the Corpus Hermeticum and these were printed in 1471. They were greeted with great enthusiasm and interest.

These documents contain information about the

Universe and spiritual teachings, which are not strange to us today, but which were regarded as heretical and dangerous by the Church authorities of the time.

A younger contemporary of Ficino, Giovanni Pico della Mirandola became strongly influenced by the Hermetic writings and combined them with his ideas on the Qabbalistic teachings and practical magic.

He wrote an oration called 'On the Dignity of Man', composed of nine hundred theses, based on Hermetic principles, which he attempted to present to the Pope, not surprisingly without success.

Heinrich Cornelius Agrippa was born on September 14, 1486 in Germany. He was a student who embraced the esoteric studies and knew many of the philosophers and writers of his time. He wrote 'Three Books on the Occult Philosophy' published in 1531, which remains one of the most outstanding studies of the subject ever written.

In 1473 in Poland Copernicus was born who, in 1543, was to put forward ideas which were to lead eventually to the establishment of the key physical laws of motion and gravity by Isaac Newton in 1687. Copernicus put forward the idea of a heliocentric Universe, placing the Sun at the centre instead of the Earth. This was an idea regarded by the Church as heretical. He took his three great ideas from the Hermetic writings. These are:

The Earth moves in space.
The Earth and planets orbit round the Sun.
The Earth rotates on its axis.

We now know these to be facts taught to every school child, but in 1473 they were revolutionary – yet they were stated clearly in these ancient Hermetic writings.

In 1548 in the Kingdom of Naples, Italy, was born one of the most remarkable minds of our history. Giordano Bruno became a Dominican monk at the age of sixteen. But he was soon studying far beyond what was acceptable to the Church. He became a dedicated disciple of the Hermetic teachings, which he believed to be Egyptian in origin, and of Qabalah, magic and astronomy. He had a prodigious memory and developed memory techniques which he claimed all could learn.

As well as the ideas of Copernicus he taught the infinite nature of the Universe, a heretical idea in his time.

Bruno wrote extensively. He travelled widely all over Europe, lecturing and writing. He was listened to by the royalty and intelligentsia of Europe, although he was not well received when he visited London.

He doubted many of the articles of dogma of the Church and then in 1592, having unwisely returned to Italy, he was betrayed by his host and arrested by the Inquisition.

He spent the next seven years in captivity, finally being burnt at the stake as a heretic on 17th February 1600.

Tommaso Campanella, a contemporary and follower of Bruno, who argued that the world is a living thing, escaped the same fate by successfully feigning insanity.

Then in 1614, a Greek scholar Isaac Casaubon claimed to prove that the Hermetic documents were not Egyptian in origin but dated from the early centuries of the Christian era and were Alexandrian Greek in origin. His opinion was to hold sway for many years and detract from the importance of the Hermetic documents. Modern opinion is however changing; it is now recognised that while the language of the Corpus Hermeticum is Alexandrian Greek, the teachings they contain can be traced back to much older Egyptian sources. Recent discoveries of ancient texts reinforce these credentials.

One of the most important English followers of the Hermetic Tradition was John Dee. Born on 13 July 1527, he was a mathematician, astronomer, astrologer, occultist, navigator, and consultant to Queen Elizabeth I. He devoted much of his life to the study of alchemy, divination and Hermetic philosophy.

One of the most learned men of his age, he had been invited to lecture on advanced algebra at the University of Paris while still in his early twenties. Dee was an ardent promoter of mathematics and a respected astronomer, as well as a leading expert in navigation, having trained many of those who would conduct England's voyages of discovery.

Dee spent much of his early adult years travelling on the continent of Europe and undoubtedly had contact with the new ideas of religion and science which were circulating in the courts and society of his time. He was misunderstood by many of his contemporaries and acquired a reputation as a somewhat dubious magician, which has dogged his reputation ever since. He was however hugely influential in establishing ideas which later emerged in the 'Rosicrucian Manifestos', the 'Fama Fraternitatis' and 'Confessio Fraternitatis', which were published in 1614 and 1615 in Germany.

These documents were greeted with immense interest and, together with the 'Corpus Hermeticum', sparked much of the spiritual change which occurred in the so-called Age of Enlightenment. New thoughts and practices flourished as Protestantism developed and grew in exoteric religion and Rosicrucianism, Freemasonry and other esoteric societies began to flourish.

Some of the distinguished followers of the Hermetic Traditions were Michael Maier (1568–1622) of Germany; Robert Fludd (1574–1637) Thomas Vaughan, 1621–1666 and Elias Ashmole (1617–1692) of England.

Through their oral tradition and ritual, modern esoteric Schools and Freemasonry continue to incorporate the teachings of the Hermetic Tradition and, though cloaked in new symbols and veiled in different metaphors, they are the modern heirs of the Tradition. Its truths live on in the teachings of the Western Mystery Tradition and several esoteric schools of the present day.

Consciousness

Consciousness is the foundation of the Universe.

This statement may seem exaggerated and unlikely. Yet if we were not conscious the Universe would not exist for us! It is only because we are conscious that we know it exists.

Consciousness is an integral part of the Created Universe: we know it exists in the human world, we see it demonstrated in the animal world, and we can imply it within what appears to us as the inanimate Universe.

Consciousness is an attribute of life. Life is an energy which flows through the whole universe.

The Universe is constantly changing, it is always in motion, it reproduces itself from the smallest cell to the greatest galaxies of the Cosmos.

In nature we see how everything changes and adapts to changing circumstances in environment. The Universe *knows* what is required. The Universe is conscious!

So let us look at the nature of consciousness in the form most familiar to us – our own experience of it.

First of all to define the terms we are using:

CONSCIOUSNESS OR CONSCIOUS
Definitions of:
1. Is characterised by having an awareness of one's own existence, sensations, and thoughts, and of one's environment. Having a particular perception; being aware.
2. Not asleep; awake.
3. Subjectively known and felt.
4. Intentionally conceived or done, deliberate.
5. Self-conscious
6. Concerned about or interested in something.

That component of waking awareness perceptible by an individual at any given instant; the conscious mind, knowing with others, participating in knowledge, aware of.

MEDICAL DEFINITION OF CONSCIOUSNESS
An awareness of self and surroundings, so that a person knows what he or she is doing and intends to do. The awareness is dependent on sensations (especially visual and auditory) memories and experiences.

Such awareness requires intact brain function, particularly within the cerebrum (the main mass of the brain) and the reticular system in the brain stem. The content of consciousness relies heavily on the functions of the cerebrum – for example, on memory and the interpretations of sensations – while wakefulness is linked with the reticular system.

Although a person may be conscious, a great deal that goes on within the brain is still below the level of consciousness. Disturbances of consciousness lead to impaired attention, concentration, and understanding. Thought processes become slowed and memory fails. There appears to be a lack of direction to thoughts and actions. Although a person can be stimulated to respond their responses are faulty.

Full consciousness is a critical awareness of one's own identity and situation.

So far we have only considered what we can call physical consciousness, of our brain and body and their functions.

However, this consciousness can be subdivided into different types of consciousness as follows, which leads us into new dimensions of the phenomena.

CONSCIOUS, SUBCONSCIOUS, PRECONSCIOUS, AND UNCONSCIOUS

These are psychological terms referring to aspects of the workings of the mind.

Conscious refers to mental processes, such as thoughts or emotional reactions, of which a person is aware.

Subconscious pertains to thoughts or feelings

outside the immediate awareness either wholly or partly.

Preconscious refers to mental processes that are outside the consciousness but are easily brought into the conscious mind.

Unconscious alludes to all mental process that a person is not aware of, including thoughts or feelings that have been forgotten or repressed, and also images, instincts, desires and the like. It is often used interchangeably with subconscious.

So there are states of consciousness in which we are not awake and aware. This seems at first sight to be a contradiction in terms.

So far the consciousness we have been considering is dependent on the body, its perceptions of the outer world about it and the inner workings of its own mind. It is physical consciousness of a material physical universe and a material brain.

Yet each night we go to sleep, we may dream while our bodies lie immobile and unaware. Yet our consciousness knows that of which we dream, it takes part in the activities of the dream and it remembers.

From the earliest of times humanity has recognised the experiences of dreams as belonging to a different type of consciousness to that of the waking world. Shamans, mystics and psychics have explored these non-physical experiences and have recorded them.

Even conventional material science recognises the structure of the Universe as being composed of unseen energy and admits its true nature as being different from how our senses perceive it.

Scientists continue to discover that Carl Jung was

right when he said "The expectation of the observer, in all experiments, produces an incalculable transformation of the data." In other words, it is becoming obvious that the expectations in the consciousness of the experimenter influences the results he obtains. So is his consciousness influencing and changing the universal consciousness in that which he is investigating?

Shamans, Mystics and Psychics say that the material world is only one of many realities, that the creative energy gives rise to many other realities which they term the spiritual or subtle worlds. They claim that these worlds can be explored - they claim to know from experience that consciousness is an effect, a manifestation of unseen energy, which manifests through the physical body but is not created by it. They claim that nonmaterial energy can be conscious, and that consciousness can exist independently of the body.

This is by no means a new idea, almost all religions have always claimed that death of the body is not the end of conscious existence – albeit of a different type to life in the body. To say there is life after death is to say that there is persistence of consciousness beyond physical death. Which is also to imply that consciousness existed prior to the creation of the body, one cannot create something immaterial which survives death through the process of physical birth.

The body undoubtedly dies, a dead body knows and feels nothing, it rapidly deteriorates and disintegrates. So if anything remains of the person it must be their consciousness.

We call this consciousness the Soul of Mankind.

Yet in an incarnate human this soul consciousness is only partially awake. It is our task to awaken the soul, to bring consciousness to its full flowering from its first stirrings to the glory of full knowledge of the total self in cosmic consciousness.

This process has been recognised at all times and in all Traditions.

In the Oriental Traditions the lotus plant was used to signify the growth of humankind through the three periods of human consciousness –

1. ignorance,
2. endeavour,
3. understanding.

A Christian interpretation of the symbol of the crucifixion is that the figure of Jesus is identified with the personal consciousness of the individual. It is this personal consciousness that conceives of and dwells in the sense of separateness, and before the aspiring soul can be reunited with the ever present and all-pervading Father, this personality must be sacrificed that the universal consciousness may be liberated.

In the Qabbalistic system it is taught how to climb the rings, that is to unfold the consciousness, through the Fifty Gates of Light, until at last one enters the Ain Soph, the Limitless Light through the Fiftieth Gate. It is said that Moses passed through the Forty-Ninth Gate but only Christ passed through the Fiftieth Gate.

The goal is to enter into conscious perception of that level of being which lies behind the manifested physical universe.

This level is pure energy, it is *conscious*, it is radiant, and it is impartial. It does not require solemnity, worship or persuasion. It does require a state of mind, which wishes only to participate in its essence, not for gain, not for ego, not for security but just to be *one* with *it* and *its* purpose.

While we are in ignorance we are, in a sense, asleep during most of our lifetimes, and possibly also while in the between life state. When we begin to awaken, we begin to strive towards understanding and our spiritual quest has begun.

All spiritual aspiration is the attempt to expand our consciousness and touch the subtle worlds while in the body.

The means and techniques by which we can achieve this entry into the sacred conscious are many and varied. Techniques with which we may be familiar are:

Meditation
Dreams
Movement
Music
Ritual

To be conscious in the subtle worlds we need to alter the focal point of our consciousness into the level we wish to contact.

It is important to remember that the language of each level is different.

It is also important to remember that we are attempting to enter into other realities - we are not attempting to have other realities enter into our material level of consciousness.

The subtle world which lies closest to the physical is the so-called astral plane. This is the level of images, words and ideas, of imagination and of pictures. For most people this world is the one we contact in dreams and meditation. It is like a mirror image of the physical plane, yet insubstantial, malleable and self-luminous.

Here we can exist in a world which looks like the physical in many ways, yet here too we can have freedom of movement and be unrestricted by time and space.

It is by being at this level that we can achieve telepathy, projection of the psychic body and nonphysical communication with others.

This level corresponds with the sphere of Yesod on the Tree of Life, which is called the Treasure House of Images.

Going deeper beyond the realm of Yesod we come into a subtle world where the language is different. Here we experience in an emotional way, we feel rather than see, this is a realm of Light where we begin to touch the Divine. It is experience of this level which gives rise to such names as the Inner Light, the Touch of the Masters, the Inner Radiance.

The experience of this level is subtle and intuitive, it is here we can know direct mind to mind contact with that Consciousness which lies even deeper in the Inner Worlds.

This level corresponds with the sphere of Tiphareth on the Tree of Life, which is called Beauty, the Son of God and the Sun behind the Sun.

Only the great Mystics and Masters have been able to penetrate deeper than this into the depths of Consciousness. We know of it only from the accounts brought back by those who have experienced it – yet one of the characteristics of these accounts is that the experience can never truly be expressed in words. The experience is ineffable, divine, supreme and life changing. For most of us, it is enough to know such worlds exist and that we too can aspire to a knowledge of them.

To be able to enter such a world by an act of will takes a great deal of practice and training, yet sometimes we do so spontaneously. It is on these occasions that we have those rare and life changing experiences which leave a permanent impression on our consciousness.

To enter the subtle worlds the first requirement is an ability to be still, to quiet the physical body, to turn the focus of awareness inwards and to maintain this state of mind for considerable periods of time. For the majority of people, modern life makes this a very difficult process; our very lifestyle leads to a short attention span and discipline of the body in a still way is not part of our modern culture. Yet this is the only doorway, the entrance is within, the key of consciousness opens the lock that guards the gateway to the subtle worlds.

A lot can be achieved by regular practice of meditation, the use of solo rituals and personal techniques.

For most people the easiest way of touching these deep realms of consciousness is in group ritual. The reason for this is because when we join together in a common focus, we become part of a group mind and share in the energies and abilities of others. The dynamics of the group mind lift us above, or deeper, than we can reach on our own, it empowers our individual consciousness with the energy of the group consciousness.

To raise our consciousness into the astral world we need to focus our awareness on something which is of the nature of that world. For this purpose, we use an image, one for which we have respect. It may be a special place, a symbol or a sacred image of a religion within which we have practised. Whatever we choose it is very important to be aware that it is something which we ourselves create from the memory banks of our own mind within our imagination. Yet a subtle transformation then takes place, the image takes on a reality of its own and becomes a vehicle by and through which we can experience within the astral realm, becoming aware of those energies which dwell within it.

Going deeper we must aspire to contact with the energies of the Divine, we must invoke a response and ask for the Great Inner Light to touch us. We should imagine a shaft of that Light reaching down towards us, perhaps filling the image we have created in the astral realm and filling and expanding our consciousness. We should act as if this has taken place – and we will find that in accordance with the measure of our sincerity and intent we will indeed be filled with an influx of something profound, sacred and life giving.

It is said that in this manner do the Initiates depart from this world. By consciously creating an astral image while in life, they enter into it, pass through and beyond it into the Greater Light and closing the door behind them no longer return to the body but go on to the next adventure in full Consciousness.

The Light Within

While I was not, as far as I know, in danger of dying, I most certainly had a near death type of out of body experience.

The experience happened many years ago when I was sixteen years of age and quite unaware that such experiences existed. It is today still clear in my memory and has had a profound effect on how I have spent my life.

I was receiving gas anaesthetic for a tooth extraction at the dentist. While this was being administered, I was aware of a kind of rotating sensation, then the sensation slowed, and I became aware I was looking at the four lights above the chair in which I was sitting. Then I realised that I was looking at them from a different angle, I was 'standing' to the right and slightly behind my physical body which I could see beside me. The dentist was standing to my left and a female assistant, who had not previously been present, was standing to the right of my body. The dentist leaned forward and lifted my right eyelid which dropped down again promptly when he released it. I knew, although it was not something I had known previously, that he was doing this to check whether I was unconscious. Then he reached to his side and lifted a pair of pliers, or dental equivalent, turning back towards me. I realised he was about to remove my tooth and felt a slight panic because I knew he thought I was unconscious. He grasped my tooth and I felt a pain but as if from a distance and not acutely. Then I thought "well that's over" and relaxed. I remember thinking that I might as well enjoy the experience I was having while I was 'there'. I seemed to move backwards rapidly and began to feel very happy and relaxed; I remember thinking that this was how it was to die and thinking it was the most marvellous feeling and nothing to be frightened about at all. Indeed, I have had no fear of death ever since, only a hope that the physical process of dying would not be painful and unpleasant.

I went deeper and deeper into a world of vast light and happiness. My consciousness seemed to expand, and I understood everything, indeed in a curious way I *was* everything. This seemed to get deeper and deeper. For a time, I dwelt in the most profound state of Light and Being. Then the thought intruded that I should go back and with the thought I began to 'descend' at speed, I felt myself approach the physical and re-entered my body through a point at the base of my head in the hollow where it joins the neck. I settled into my body like waking from sleep to hear the dentist saying in tones of great relief "she is coming around, she is smiling". When I opened my eyes, he said "where have you been? I have had a real struggle bringing you round." I was about to tell him I had just had the most wonderful experience, but something stopped me and I was silent. I felt perfectly alright and had no aftereffects.

In later times when I read of the sudden unexpected death of someone under a dental anaesthetic I wondered if the same thing happened and the soul personality either chose not to or could not return.

In the following years I tried to repeat the experience at will but have never achieved it to any depth, there was always a feeling it was not right to do so and an inexplicable slight fear of succeeding! But I have always known that I was given the experience to awaken me and to teach me what I would, in future times, teach others - that we are conscious beings who live in, but are not dependent on, a physical vehicle. When the time comes I know I will once again return to and dwell in that state which is so much more conscious, so much more vivid, so much more alive and so much more knowing and wiser than that I am familiar with as my physical self.

I have since experienced being conscious on that plane which lies just beyond the physical, which is like a mirror image of it, where one can walk through walls, do physically impossible things and have significant experiences in dreams and deep meditation, and on rare occasions experienced deeper into the Inner Light. But I have never since penetrated again to that realm of Light which lies far beyond the so-called astral plane.

Solo Opening and Closing Ritual

REQUIREMENTS

A secure and private small space
Small table for altar (round or square/oblong) and comfortable but not easy chair
Cloth to cover altar
Four small candles
Matches
Candle snuffer
Taper
Music player if desired

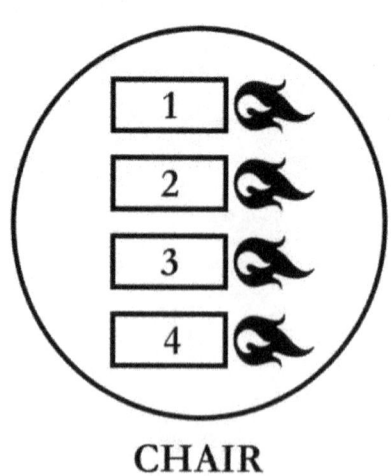

CHAIR

RITUAL

OPENING

Prepare the Temple as depicted in the diagram above.
Prepare yourself by washing hands and face.
Wear a plain ritual robe if desired.
Enter the temple and bow the head to the altar in recognition of its sacredness.

Taking lit taper, stand facing the altar
Be silent for a few minutes to still the mind then light the first candle while saying
> *Almighty Creative Powers,*
> *fill this place with Thy power and blessing.*

Light second candle while saying
> *Holy Powers of Knowledge and of Wisdom,*
> *teach me that I may grow.*

Light third candle while saying
> *Guides of the Inner Worlds,*
> *bless my inner journeys that I may learn.*

Light fourth candle while saying
> *Sacred Powers of Earth,*
> *bless my earthly life and my spiritual quest.*

Bow to the altar and be seated. Proceed with any work which is desired.

CLOSING

When the work is completed, spend few minutes in meditation of thanks.
Rise and stand in from of altar, taking candle snuffer.

Extinguish the first candle saying:
*Almighty Creative Powers,
I thank you for your influence in this place.*
Extinguish the second candle saying
*Holy Powers of Knowledge and of Wisdom,
make clear my memory of your teachings.*
Extinguish the third candle saying
*Guides of the Inner Worlds,
accept my thanks and keep me in the knowledge of the inner ways.*
Extinguish the fourth candle saying
*Sacred Powers of Earth,
bless my earthly life and my spiritual quest.*

Bow to the altar and depart.

Disrobe and spend a little time in silence. Take something to eat and drink.

Magical Worlds

Prepare yourself and your environment for visualisation as you would normally do so.

As you sit comfortably and peacefully, become aware of your surroundings in an intense way. Feel the chair beneath you, the floor under your feet, the temperature of the room, the sounds and even the vague scents of your physical environment. Focus into these sensations, register them, then let them go.

Now turn your attention to your own bodily

sensations. Are you comfortable? If not, attend to any discomforts so that you can allow your body to relax and let your attention be removed from the physical-material world for a short time.

Now examine your thinking. Are stray thoughts distracting you? If so deal with them and let them go. Do not try to force the mind into stopping thinking, just allow any small thoughts to drift by rather than holding your attention.

The world of the mind is your own particular kingdom, your private retreat. Here you may think exactly what you please in total privacy.

For a short time I am going to ask you to let me take you into a world of shared imagination so that together we may enter those very deep levels of the mind where it becomes possible to communicate with each other and enter a shared inner world.

You find yourself standing in front of a door. Note its shape and texture, and any distinctive features there may be. Then look at the centre of the door, just at eye level, where you can see your own initials embossed or engraved.

Push the door gently. It will swing open to your touch, then go through the door allowing it to swing softly closed behind you.

You are standing on a pathway in a tall beech wood. The trees tower high above your head. You can see the sunlight flickering through the thinning foliage. It is autumn and there is already a rich carpet of golden leaves about your feet. The ground rises on either side of you and you realise you are in a shallow valley.

The path rises ahead of you and disappears behind some tall bushes on the top of the rise.

You decide to follow the path and soon come to the edge of the beech wood.

The path continues upwards through tall rhododendron bushes. It becomes so steep that a set of small steps has been cut into the hillside to ease the climb, It is an effort to reach the top but suddenly you are there.

You emerge onto a grassy hilltop on the top of which is a small tower. It is three stories high with narrow windows set deep into the stonework. You notice a small wooden door at the base of the tower, which is just ajar. You decide to enter and explore.

Pushing the door fully open you go inside. At first it is too dark to see, but as your eyes become accustomed to the gloom you find yourself in a small, empty, circular chamber about twelve feet in diameter. Across the room you see a small opening which appears to lead to a narrow staircase.

With slightly pounding heart you cross the room and begin to climb the stairs, which wind round and round. You come out into another room, a duplicate of the one on the ground floor. The tower seems to be completely empty. So you continue the climb to the next floor.

Reaching the top you step out into another chamber – and here stop dead in your tracks with surprise. In the centre of the room stands the tall figure of a man. He wears a long red robe and appears to be contemplating the objects on a table in front of him. The room is comfortably furnished, and a profusion of flowers soften the stern look of the tower's interior.

Your eyes return once more to the man. Slowly he glances up at you with no sign of surprise at your presence. Then he smiles slightly and beckons you forward.

As you get nearer to the table you recognise the objects upon it. There is an earthen platter, a wooden staff, a beautiful finely wrought chalice and a long slender sword with strange devices engraved upon the hilt. You look up into the man's eyes, recognising him as the Magician of the Tarot. He nods in acknowledgement as he notes your understanding.

Gently he takes your arm and guides you towards a second door which you had not noticed. He opens it and invites you to step through.

You find yourself standing on a small flat roof. surrounded by a very strong looking wall which is sufficiently high to make you feel safe and secure.

The Magician bids you look out over the surrounding countryside. You do so and are amazed at the variety of scenery which meets your eyes. In one direction the land looks lush and fertile, in another it is bare and barren, as if it had been long neglected or subject to some great catastrophe which had stripped it bare. In yet another direction the land is spring green with new growth and bright with fresh blossom.

The Magician tells you that the land you see below you is the land of your own inner country. He bids you note the places where it needs your attention and care, and tells you to rejoice at the beauty of the well-tended and lived in places. Look well at this landscape and make note of those places which

Journeys in the Light Within

require your attention. Look well and remember.

After you have spent some time concentrating on your inner landscape, a gentle touch on your arm brings your attention back to the Magician. He indicates that it is time for you to leave the roof of the tower and you turn and follow him inside.

With a brief yet not unkindly nod, he dismisses you and you turn and once more descend the staircase. Soon you are outside the tower once more and look about you, wondering which way to go next. Then you see a small path; it is steep, but you decide to take it and see where it leads.

Presently you are again walking among tall bushes, but gradually they become more orderly and cultivated and you find yourself walking in a beautiful garden. On either side there are flowering bushes of all kinds, beds of heather, blooms of every season in an improbable blaze of colour and beauty, and framing the scene ancient trees stand guardian on either side.

On your left hand there is a small stream which glitters in the sunlight. The path continues to gently descend. Every now and then the stream has been dammed into small pools on which float lilies of every variety and colour. You notice the swift flash of brightly coloured fishes as they dart here and there among the reeds and other plants of the pools.

It is so beautiful here and you feel you could spend forever in this calm, healing soothing atmosphere. Time seems suspended as you enjoy the beauty and feel your inner being responding to the visual beauty, the sounds of the birds and the soft rustles of small creatures in the undergrowth.

You have lingered longer than you intended, and it is the sound of footsteps which bring you back to an awareness of passing time. Down the path behind you come a young couple, hand in hand. They are engrossed in each other and their faces shine with happiness and youth. As they come level with you, they smile at you and give you greeting. They pause for a moment and you recognise in them a reflection of all your own youthful hopes and zest for life. They smile at you and go on, feeling rejuvenated and happy, remembering and recapturing that intense feeling of love of life.

As you walk down the hill, the trees come closer, and the garden gives way to the wood and autumn leaves once more rustle about your feet.

Suddenly you reach the end of the trees and step out onto a grassy pasture. Before you is the most beautiful and tranquil scene. The grass slopes gently down to a small lake whose absolutely calm waters reflect, as in a perfect mirror, the hillsides which surround it. You stand at the water's edge entranced by the beauty of this place. Suddenly the absolute calm of the water is broken as if a small wind has suddenly ruffled its surface, but there is no wind and in any case the disturbance of the water is confined to one small area. Your heart jumps in alarm as something suddenly appears above the water.

From the water slowly rises a beautiful woman, her long hair floating on the water as she emerges, and her thin green gown clinging closely about her perfect form. In her hands she holds a silver chalice, filled to the brim with the water of the lake. She walks straight towards you across the surface and offers the chalice to you. She bids you drink, for these waters are totally pure and have the ability to heal and cleanse all manner of hurts and ills. You accept the chalice from her hands and drink deep of its cool sweet contents.

The woman comes to stand beside you, and you return the chalice to her hands. She bids you look into the lake and tells you that its waters are of unknown depths. When the surface is calm, you can still see into it as in a mirror and it will reveal to you the secrets of your deepest self. It will instruct and guide you if you but ask to see. She bids you look well and remember.

You spend a few minutes gazing into the water, then slowly whatever images you've been contemplating fade away. You see only the calm surface of the lake. The lady is nowhere to be seen and only the soft call of a solitary bird over the water breaks the silence.

After one last long look at the mirror image of the mountains in the water, you retrace your steps up the grassy slope towards the trees. As you enter their shady protection you feel more relaxed and at peace than you can remember feeling for a long time. The dappled sunshine coming through the high treetops lights the path before you. You walk slowly along until you realise you are once more in the beech wood with the autumn leaves rustling softly in the slight breeze. Then the path comes to an end and before you is the door with your initials upon it. As you touch it the door swings open gently and you pass through it, closing it behind you. Slowly you become aware once more of your physical self, the feel of the floor beneath your feet in the physical world and the sounds about you in the room where you sit. Gently move, stretch

and come back to full wakefulness.
   End the work as your normally would.

The Tree of Life

The Qabbalistic Tree of Life is a symbol of the creation and energies of the Universe. It describes the process by which our material and spiritual worlds, and our self, come into being.

The Qabalah comes from the ancient Jewish tradition of mystical interpretation of the Bible, first transmitted orally and using esoteric methods (including ciphers). It reached the height of its influence in the later Middle Ages and remains significant in Hasidism. The modern symbol of the Tree of Life first appeared in 1516. It is based on the descriptions in the Jewish book of the 'Sepher Yetzirah'. It has developed into the one we use today in many of the modern esoteric schools. So let us explore its meaning.

We start with the great unmanifest, the sphere we call Kether. This is chaos from our point of view, it is creative power which is unlimited, unformed and timeless. It has no existence in any form we can imagine or realise. It just *is*. Kether is the great unity - the One.

Kether sends out a wave which splits into two rates of vibration. These are the basic polarities of the Universe and Creation. We recognise them as plus and minus, male and female, light and dark. They are neither good nor evil, they simply *are*.

We name these energies Chokmah and Binah.

Chokmah is the positive pole, it is the source of the positive/masculine side of creation.

Binah is the negative pole, it is the source of the negative/feminine side of creation.

It is important not to think of Binah's energy as negative, in the sense of earthly negativity. It is merely the opposite pole to the positive Chokmah.

The creative force flows onwards and at the next level the first ideas of form are created. This is the sphere of Chesed.

This is as yet not form as we know it but the archetypal idea of it.

Within Chesed the ideas, laws and frameworks of the Universe are laid down.

On the opposite sphere on the Tree to Chesed is Geburah. Here are formed the forces which break down and change everything.

The next level down we call Tiphareth. At this level the force begins to express a spiritual energy. This is the cradle of the soul. For humanity, in its attempts to rise to the spiritual levels, this is the highest it is possible to attain. This sphere is the level of the gods of humanity. It is the sacred and the holy.

Below Tiphareth we come to the spheres of Netzach and Hod.

Netzach holds the energies that animate the life force. Here are the patterns of desires and loves, hates and dislikes, the love of the beautiful and all art and emotion.

Hod holds the energies which create the intellect. These forces enable us to acquire knowledge and create our world.

Now we descend to the sphere of Yesod, the sphere of the unconscious mind. Here are formed the laws which govern life. We touch this level in dreams and meditation.

Finally, the creative force reaches Malkuth, the sphere of manifestation. Here is our cosmic universe, solar systems and earthly life. Everything we call material exists in Malkuth, from the smallest atom to the largest galaxy.

This is the basic pattern of the Tree of Life. In addition, there are the pathways which link the spheres together, each of which expresses particular powers.

It should also be stated that there are four levels to the Tree expressed as four worlds each of which contains its own Tree.

The process begins in Atziluth which is pure force
|
Briah pure ideas and archetypal pattern.
|
Yetzirah astral spiritual energies
|
Assiah the manifest physical universe.

Journeys in the Light Within

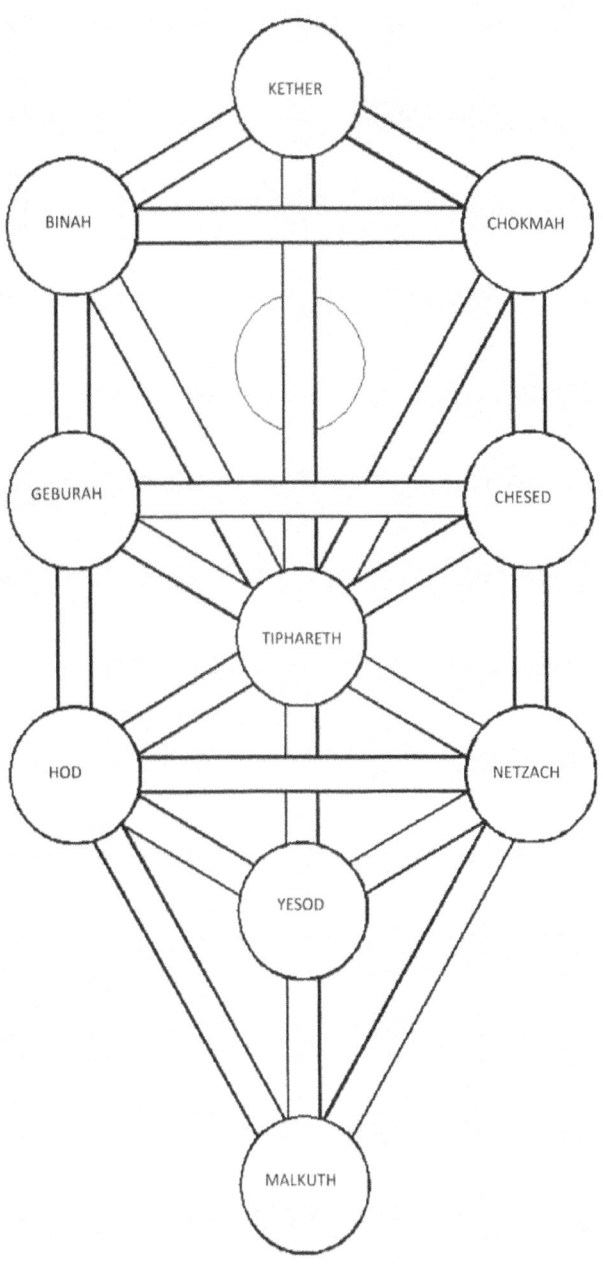

Magical Bridges

Prepare yourself and your environment for visualisation as you would normally do so.

As you relax and close your eyes, breathe deeply and slowly.

Gradually, you begin to see a scene unfold before your inner eye. There is a pathway before you, which leads you beneath a beautiful stone archway. Follow the path which takes you through a pleasant sunlit garden.

Gradually the formal cultivated garden gives way to woodland. Trees of every kind and colour grow in this woodland, and small creatures go about their business, oblivious to your passing.

Journeys in the Light Within

Your path leads you deeper and deeper into the wood, as you make you make a slow descent to lower ground.

You walk at a leisurely pace for some time, enjoying the peaceful quiet atmosphere of the wood. Quite suddenly the trees come to an end and you find yourself looking out over a large lake. The sunlight shimmers on the quiet water and small ripples reflect the light in a thousand dancing diamonds of brilliance.

As you look out across the lake, you see through a bright haze, the trees and broad grassland of the further shore. Here there are again formal gardens and you can just see the outline of a large house among the trees with a broad grassed avenue sweeping down to the lakeside.

To your left the pathway continues along the side of the lake and you continue to follow it, to your left the tall trees of the woodland, and to your right, at the edge of the water, graceful bulrushes and irises bend gently in a slight breeze.

Water birds rise in momentary alarm as you pass but soon settle back to their quiet pursuits as you continue on your way.

Eventually you reach a bend in the path and find yourself standing before two majestic trees, mighty sentinels that guard the path ahead. You look with awe at the immense trunks of the trees, which are several feet in diameter, and above your head the interlacing patterns of branch and leaf give glimpses of sun and sky and the top of the trees some several hundred feet above your head.

You see the figure of a young girl standing just

beyond the trees, the hue of her soft green dress blending into the woods behind her and the bright gold of her hair seeming to be but another beam of sunlight shining through the trees. She smiles as she sees you've become aware of her presence and beckons you to follow her.

Once past the guardian trees, you notice a subtle change in the view before you – colours glow more vividly and the sunlight seems to have a kind of self-luminous quality. Before you stretches once more the waters of the lake but through a haze which yet does not obscure your view.

Following your guide you come to the water's edge and see before you a small island in the lake. Its form is indistinct, there are trees and flashes of bright colour as if many flowers bloom in its gardens, yet you cannot see more than brief impressions. You feel a great desire to visit the island but you wonder how to reach it. Then, as you watch, before your startled eyes, the transparent outline of a bridge begins to form. In a graceful arch it stretches from the ground at your feet, out across the water and appears to end on the shores of the beckoning island.

Your young guide steps upon the bridge and indicates that you should follow her. With some hesitation you step out onto the bridge; it is a strange feeling to see nothing substantial beneath your feet and yet you know that the bridge will take you safely across the water. Initially the island appeared to be quite close, yet as you continue on the bridge you seem to be walking for some time.

Before you forms a deep red mist and you walk forward until it surrounds you. You look for your guide, but it is no longer the figure of a young girl - the folds of a dark red cloak now cover the figure of a mature man. He turns to face you and you see his strong face, his features are full of wisdom and despite his grey beard there is an air of vitality about him. He smiles at you and says: "Welcome to the Rainbow Bridge which will take you from your world of physical reality to the inner place of refreshment and discovery. Here in the red light of the rainbow you can let go of all the cares, worries, disappointments and sorrows of the outer world. In this light you can see that all experiences of Earth have their own purposes and reasons. Here you can leave all that causes you grief or sorrow and take with you only that which you have gained from those experiences." He smiles at you again then stretches out his arms to you as if embracing all you would discard, then turns and walks on. You feel the red mist swirling about you and like a great cleansing fire, you feel it sweep away all cares and regrets.

    Walking forward you notice the light changing and brightening until you are enveloped in a bright glowing mist of vivid orange. The Guide still walks ahead of you, but his dark red cloak has changed to a long robe of purest white with a loose over-cloak of bright orange. There are other changes too, no longer is his hair grey with years but rich, dark and bright with the sheen of youth. No sooner do you notice his changed appearance than your Guide stops and turns once more towards you. His features have the same strength in every line, yet they are those of a man in the full strength of his young maturity. In his hand he holds a shining sword, unsheathed, which gleams and glitters as it catches the light.

"Welcome to the Orange light of the Rainbow Bridge", he says. "Here you may come to know the hidden powers of your mind. This is the realm of imagination and vision, here are those images formed which are the foundation of creation, and yours is the sword of will which guides and rules their birth." Lifting high his sword he holds it momentarily high above you as if in benediction, then although you do not see him move - he is no longer there.

Gradually the orange light fades and changes and as you walk forward you are enveloped in a brilliant blazing yellow light. It is as if the very air about you shines with living gold.

Then from the light as through a golden haze there comes a woman, tall and beautiful. Blue as the sky of heaven is her robe and on her brow a diadem of stars. "Welcome to the yellow light of the Rainbow Bridge", she says and stretches out her hands as if to clasp your own. "Here you may rest in peace and warm security for I will bring you gifts of inner joy. In this light is seen the truth of nature's laws, the cycles of the seasons and the stars. Place in my hand the longing of your heart and I will take your secrets for my own." So saying she spreads her cloak wide as if to embrace you and, like a child, you go to her.

Slowly as if waking from deep sleep you once again become aware of light, but now the hue is green as forest glade. A regal figure now stands before your eyes, his rich dark cloak is ermine trimmed and on his brow there gleams a circlet of pure gold. "Welcome to the green light of the Rainbow Bridge", he says. His voice is deep and strong and full of quiet authority.

Journeys in the Light Within

"Now is the time for you to know your sovereignty, to recognise no other ruler of yourself. This is the knowledge which the green light brings, that only you may rule the inner realms of yourself. Touch of my sceptre brings this gift to you that you may rule yourself in wisdom, strength and peace." Then stretching forth the sceptre in his hand, it seems he touches you upon the brow. A wave of power sweeps through you from his hand and deep within you feel yourself enthroned and crowned.

Then once more you see the bridge on which you stand and realise that now the gentle curve it forms no longer rises but at last descends.

The light has changed through subtle shift of hue and now you walk in a deep, sea blue, swirling with strange shapes and shades of dreams and visions from the hidden depths of your mind. From these swirling images a figure forms, a woman tall and radiating power. Her robe of midnight blue is blazoned with strange symbols at her breast and sweeps with regal majesty about her feet. Upon her head a moon disc blazes with pale light supported by the horns of Hathor's sign.

You meet her eyes and in their depths you recognise authority borne in Light. She raises both her hands, palms facing you, on level with her eyes and says, "Welcome to the blue light of the Rainbow Bridge. Here is the door which opens to the Moon, to inner realms which lie between the worlds. In this light can you find an inner peace and walk within the wisdom of the Gods. This is the place of granting of your hearts desires, here you may see with eyes no longer veiled, here you may pass beyond the ties of

Earth and know yourself approaching your true home."

Then from her hands a power flows and opens wide the eye within the mind that you may see and understand.

The blue mist darkens as if night falls, then as you watch the female figure slowly disappears and in her place there stands a man in robe so dark you cannot see its hue.

"Welcome to the indigo light of the Rainbow Bridge", he says in a voice in which there are echoes of command. His presence fills you with a deep sense of reverence and of awe yet there is a warmth which embraces you.

"Come follow me into the violet light that we may reach that place which lies beyond the bridge."

With some relief you follow him, glad that soon you will once more stand on solid ground. You walk through the dark violet light, suddenly the island is beneath your feet and you emerge, dazzled into the full brilliance of the daylight. A path appears before you and just ahead you see the figure of your Guide now clothed in robes of purest white. You hurry to follow before he goes beyond your sight and find yourself walking through gardens of great beauty and tranquillity.

You follow the path for a little time then see before you on a little hill, a small open Temple whose snow white pillars gleam in the brightness of the noonday sun and whose roof of silver reflects its bright beams back high into the sky. As you approach you see there are three shallow steps which lead you up into the sanctuary, you walk up the steps to approach the

Journeys in the Light Within

central altar made of white stone. Upon the altar is a wide deep dish filled with crystal clear water to the brim and from the centre of the water leaps a flame, a living light whose source you cannot see. Then as you stand, spellbound at the sight, a vision forms within the water's depth.

You see your deepest hopes and hearts desires, you see the answers you have sought so long, you see the hidden secrets and lock the knowledge deep within your heart.

Smiling, your Guide receives you as you leave and bids you sit in silence underneath the trees. Gratefully you sink into the soft reclining seats and let yourself remember what you have seen. Then on the air there comes a ringing sound which swells and grows across the isle and lake. The sound ends, blending into silence and once more your Guide bids you rise and follow him.

You feel a touch of sadness as you rise, knowing your time here now is drawing to a close. Following your Guide you come once more to the lakeside and see before you the Rainbow Bridge, but now no mists obscure its shape and you can see it curving to the farther shore.

Thanking your Guide, who bids you here farewell, you step once more upon the bridge. You see the water of the lake clear beneath your feet and watch the golden fish dart quickly out of view. It is not far and soon you have crossed and you step upon the shore and woodland path. Slowly you make your way back along the path the Way you came.

Then before you is the beautiful stone arch and passing through you find yourself once more aware of your body in the room, then stretch and open your eyes and come back to outer consciousness.

Demeter and Persephone

A Visualisation in the Style of a Spiritual Drama from Classical Times

The Storyteller parts may be divided amongst a group or read by one person.

The Storytellers:

Narrator
Demeter
Zeus
Persephone
Hades
Zeus
Ascalaphus

NARRATOR - In the beginning of time when the world was young and the gods still walked upon earth, the land and the sky and the depths of the sea were one with their heavenly homes.

Gods walked upon the earth in those times, they loved and fought, developed their powers and their domains, and created story and myth which still lives down to our day.

DEMETER - I, Demeter, saw a barren world, new born from fire and ice. Dark was its face and no living things were there upon its breast. Death it knew not, for death is the other face of life and life was not yet born upon the earth.

My mother, Rhea, was the earth, and my Father was her brother, Cronus, Lord of Time. I, being daughter of the gods, was stirred to compassion for the lifeless earth and into my hands was given the power of creating growing things.

With the touch of my finger I caused the green grass to grow, the trees to rise towards the heavens, fruits and flowers to come forth in rich profusion and the face of earth to become beautiful and bountiful. Then were all living things created. For humankind I caused the corn and grape to grow that they might be sustained and nourished there-from.

I walked in this fair garden and my heart rejoiced to see it flourish in rich fertility. All creatures found their mates and brought forth their young. The plants blossomed and sent forth seeds and all living things reproduced their kind.

Yet had I no mate to bring such joy to me.

ZEUS - I, Zeus, the Father of Heaven, am brother to fair Demeter, but husband also to my sister Hera. Yet my sister Demeter was young and fair and I made with her a daughter, Core, who later was named Persephone, who is the beloved of her mother's heart.

PERSEPHONE - I, Persephone, rejoiced in the love of my mother and shared with her the tending of earths plants and all green and growing things.

My days were carefree, and I knew no fear nor pain but only the kiss of the sun and the laughter of the maids who were my companions. In the fair meadows we danced and sang and wove bright garlands from the flowers, which matched the rainbow in their dazzling hues.

HADES - I am Hades, my realm is the dark land of Tartarus beneath the earth. My land is one of soft shadows, of dark pools and hidden places. No noisy calls of bird or beast disturb the silence of my halls. No glittering sunlight, nor the raucous noise of life, weary the eye and ear within my kingdom. Lord of the Underworld am I called. My subjects are those who have departed from the life of earth and my powers are those of the hidden fires, of earthquake, chasms and the treacherous deeps.

One day, in my dark chariot, I drove with my four fiery coal black steeds, to oversee the molten rivers of my volcanic fires. Returning I heard a song upon the wind and girlish laughter lured me on to seek its source. The fairest maid that ever god could see, I found to be the singer of the song. One glance at her sweet loveliness and grace and all my solitude and peace was bitter loneliness and pain. This maid held all my hope of happiness and I knew I must possess her or know no rest again.

So to my brother Zeus I went to seek the hand of this fair maid that I might take her for my lawful wife.

ZEUS - Then to my court came Hades, the fond suitor of Persephone and asked me for her hand in sacred marriage. How to refuse my brother god his wish? Yet should I consent, the wrath of Demeter would bring her unforgiving enmity upon me - for she would never agree to her beloved daughter being committed to dark Tartarus.

So I answered that I could neither give nor withhold my consent and left the matter unresolved for fear of whom I would offend.

HADES - The goddesses had all refused to share my throne, poured scorn and derision on my suit, not one would be my consort and my queen. So was I left in lonely solitude. Now Zeus would not give his favour to my suit of fair Persephone.

I vowed that no more would I go wooing for a willing wife - but take the one I now desired and by my force would bend her to my will.

Since Zeus would not decide and grant me Persephone to wife, I swore that I would have her - unwilling and without his blessing.

PERSEPHONE - Upon a day most fair, my maids and I plucked blossoms in a tranquil meadow on a mountain side. The sun was warm, the breeze a sweet delight, the world a place of happiness and peace. We danced and sang all unaware of the dark shadow threatening my innocence.

The noise of crackling branches and hasty footsteps made us swiftly turn, straight from the bushes strode a dark visaged intruder of lowering countenance, direct to where I sat, he strode and - horror of horrors - seized me in his brawny arms. My maidens stood in frozen fear and before I, or they, could do ought to save me from my fate, he swept me up and bore me screaming to his chariot. My prayers and struggles were to no avail, but only served to make him urge his fiery steeds to greater speed, and soon the cries and lamentations of my maids were lost to me as I to them.

HADES - Faster and faster I drove my steeds, eager to have my sweet treasure safe within my realm, before Demeter should become aware of her loss and force me to relinquish her again. The very trees reached out to tear her from my grasp, the rivers seethed and roared in flood to block my path, but I was not to be thwarted of my prize.

I raised my two-pronged fork high in the air and struck the earth a mighty blow - then the earth split wide and a great chasm opened at my feet, through which my chariot, horses, Persephone and I plunged down into the darkness of the lower world.

PERSEPHONE - Alas, alas, my tears and lamentations were of no avail. Dark Hades held me fast and rescue or escape were impossible. I saw the earth gape wide and knew myself now doomed to hells dark halls. Yet ere the earth could close above my head, I tore the girdle from about my waist and flung it into the waters of the roaring flood that some water nymph might catch it and carry it to my mother for a clue.

HADES - Once safe within my realm, I clasped my fair young captive to my breast, pressed kisses on her cheek and lip and sought to calm her panic and her fear. At last we reached the comfort of my halls. I took my fair Persephone to be my own, made of her my woman and my queen.

I seated her upon my throne and saw that all paid honour to her place. Yet did my fair queen still weep and grieve and though the richest foods my table held, still did she refuse to eat and daily I watched her brightness fade.

DEMETER - On that dark day I lost my love of life, all youthful carefree days were at an end. Returning from the fields of ripening grain, I sought the joyful welcome in my house. But no sweet words of welcome met my ears, no loving arms to greet me at the close of day. Empty and cold was my dwelling place and though I called and called no daughter came to bid me welcome home.

I sought her maids that they might tell me of her, but when I found them they but added to my grief with garbled tales of monsters from the deep.

I met with old Hecate on the way and she gave me news which but added to my grief. She said that on that day she heard a maiden scream and cry "a rape, a rape" but hurrying to the spot she found no trace of her.

From place to place I sought Persephone, asking all who would listen to tell me of her fate. But I knew no more after nine long agonising days. It seemed she had vanished from the earth and left no clue, nor trace, to ease my heart.

So, distraught with grief and loss, I wandered over hill and dale, my daily tasks neglected and undone; the rain uncalled to wash the drooping flowers, the grain all parched and grass all perished from the unremitting sun, all green and growing things wilted and died for want of my previous care.

At last I came to Eleusis and there I learnt from a shepherd how his brother, a swineherd, had been out in the fields on the day Persephone was lost. When the earth had suddenly gaped open, engulfing his swine before his very eyes. Then had he seen a chariot, drawn by fiery black horses, which dashed down the mighty chasm and disappeared. He could not see the face of the chariot driver but in his right arm, tightly clasped, was a weeping shrieking girl.

I knew then with awful certainty the identity of the charioteer.

Alas! - for my beloved Persephone, stolen and held against her will by Hades in his dark realms of Tartarus.

I hastened back to where she last was seen and searched in vain for some entry to her prison. Then one day, while wandering on a riverbank, the waters suddenly cast a glittering object at my feet. It was the girdle my daughter wore, that last day before she was torn from me.

I summoned Hecate and together we approached the mighty Helios, who sees everything, and forced him to admit that Hades was indeed the guilty one.

NARRATOR - Now Demeter sunk ever deeper in her grief, convinced that Hades would never now release Persephone. She withdrew into a dark cave to mourn unseen and still further neglected her wonted duties.

Famine now threatened the land and the people prayed and clamoured for Demeter's aid. But she in anger and unremitting grief forbade the trees to yield fruit and the herbs to grow. She swore that nothing on earth would grow with her permission, as long as her daughter was detained in the underworld by Hades.

Despair walked the land and the people cried long to Zeus that he should force Hades to free Persephone and reunite her with her mother that fertility might once more blossom in the land.

ZEUS - I listened to the supplications of the people and knew that what they said was all too true. The earth was dying fast.

So I sent a message to Demeter and when I received no reply I sent a deputation of the gods who bore her gifts and begged her to be reconciled to my will and once more do her duties to the land. But all to no avail, Demeter was deaf to all my pleas. Then I sent swift Hermes with a message to Hades bidding him say to him that he must restore Persephone to her mother or the world was doomed.

And to Demeter I sent a message saying that I would order Persephone to be freed on the single condition that she had not eaten of the food of the dead while she had resided at Hades court.

Journeys in the Light Within

HADES - I longed to keep Persephone with me, but since no morsel of food had passed her lips since I had brought her to my world, I could not refuse the edict of great Zeus. So hiding the rage within my heart, I spoke to her in soft and gentle words to turn what must be done to my own best advantage. I said to her that I had seen she was not happy in my realm and that I knew her mother wept ceaselessly for her return. So I would send her home and set her free.

PERSEPHONE - My heart leapt high when Hades told me I could go - to see the deep blue sky, to smell the grass and flowers, to eat the fruits of earth and feel the fresh wind blow upon my face. These things for which I had wept so long would soon once again be mine. In my relief and gratitude I almost felt a small affection for this unwanted spouse of mine.

ASCALAPHUS - But not so easily would the fair Persephone escape. I, Ascalaphus, gardener in Tartarus, had that day, all unbeknown to her, watched as she held a pomegranate in her hand. She opened up the fruit and as it spoke to her of sunlit days, she picked a seed and touched it to her lips. Seven seeds I saw her eat. I will bear witness for my Lord that Persephone has tasted the food of the dead and therefore, cannot in truth, claim her freedom be granted under the conditions of great Zeus.

HADES - At this most welcome news I sought to detain Persephone still within my halls, but Hermes did insist I give her up and submit the matter to the judgment of my brother Zeus. So I gave Persephone into his care - but bid Ascalaphus to ride also on Hermes' chariot that he might bear witness for me before Zeus of the eating of the pomegranate seeds, and thus bring Persephone back to me.

DEMETER - Ah- that such joy and sorrow should meet in the same breath. I held my beloved daughter once more in my arms, but bitterness came swift upon my joy, for Ascalaphus came to speak for Hades before Zeus, and declared that Persephone had eaten while in the halls of Hades and therefore must return.
   I swore that if indeed Zeus sent her back then would I be for ever an exile from Olympus and never would I remove my curse from off the land.

ZEUS - Now did all seem lost, for Demeter and Hades both would have their way and thus the matter would never be resolved. So seeking wisdom greater than my own I sought the council of our mother Rhea, that she might persuade Demeter to lift her curse and allow the land once more to bloom. But her appeals met answer as my own.
   Until of my mother's wisdom a compromise was found, which Demeter and Hades would both agree to keep and honour, though neither willingly conceded Persephone to the other.

NARRATOR - Thus Zeus decreed. Because she had tasted of the food of the dead, Persephone must remain the wife of Hades and sit at his side as Queen of Tartarus, so was Hades granted his desire.
Because Persephone had only partaken of the seeds of the pomegranate, for half of each year she must live

in Tartarus, but for the remainder of the year she would be free to live in the sunlight on the bright earth with her mother Demeter. Thus was Demeter granted her desire.

So Zeus appointed Hecate to watch over Persephone and to see that she observed his decree. To Hermes he gave the task of leading Persephone to and from Hades. Whenever he brought her out of her gloomy prison, the skies became blue and sunny, the grass sprang fresh and green beneath her feet and flowers bloomed in joy along her way. All nature sprang to new life to welcome her home once more.

Demeter, once again happy in the company of her beloved daughter, returned to her duties and blessed the earth with plenty. The earth was green once more, the corn grew, the grapes were heavy on the vines and all life flourished.

But when once more the time for the departure of Persephone drew near, again the skies wept and all nature mourned. While she was absent, Demeter mourned beyond consolation and the earth lay barren and cold. Only Hades was happy in these months, Persephone sat sad-faced and pale at his side with only the knowledge of her coming reunion with her mother to comfort her.

But the dark days passed, Hermes came once more and Persephone and Demeter were reunited and blessed the land again with their joy.

So has it been since the earth was young, so will it be until the bright sun fades, so will it be while the great ones reign, so will it be until the end of time.

Being

A Visualisation Exercise

Begin by sitting in a comfortable chair, relax.

Now concentrate on your body, feel the chair supporting you, your feet on the ground, your hands on your lap.

Be aware of the clothes you are wearing, where they fit tight or loose.

Notice any sounds or scents of which you may be aware.

Close your eyes and for a few moments just focus on these sensations within your body.

What colours do you see or sense?

Now turn your attention to that part of your mind

that is observing these sensations.

Where do you feel this sense of awareness is centred in your body?

Wherever this point may be feel it as the point from which your consciousness radiates.

Now in the centre of this point see a pinpoint of violet light, if you have difficulty seeing it just feel it. Allow the violet light to expand and grow until it fills all your area of consciousness.

Imagine you are getting sleepy, you are almost about to cross the borderline and begin to dream. Be aware of your mind dreaming, these images are arising from your sub-conscious. Just let them form and dissolve, do not try to control them or form any particular pictures or patterns.

See if you can move your point of consciousness into this dreaming part of your mind so that you feel as if you are living in and observing the dreaming as you do the waking world.

Again, in the centre of your point of consciousness there forms a point of light, it is warm and golden like a miniature sun. Allow this golden light to expand and grow until it fills the whole of your consciousness.

In this light you ARE only your point of consciousness, your body is resting and does not require your attention just now.

Allow yourself to BE the golden light. This light is that mysterious inner radiance which permeates all creation, it is the light which is also the energy from which matter and astral forms are made.

Now in the centre of the golden light see a tiny pinpoint of brilliant white light, it is very, very intense and pure.

Gradually the pinpoint grows until your whole consciousness is flooded with its brilliance.

As you allow the light to grow you realise that you ARE this light, it is your soul essence, it is your greater Self. It is this light which you have been from the beginning and it is your connection to the Divine Light.

Feel yourself both being and radiating the light and also feel it flooding into you from the source of light deep within creation.

For a time remain in the light and allow it to warm and strengthen your inner being, your point of consciousness.

(*a few minutes of silence*)

It is time for us to leave this inner place. Draw the light back into a point and allow it to fade seeing yourself once more in the golden light.

Slowly draw the golden light back into a point and allow it to fade. The violet light once more surrounds you.

Now draw the violet light back into a point and allow it to fade.

Gently feel your body about you, move and become aware of the room around you.

Now open your eyes.

The Inner Self

PART ONE

You are standing before an old high wall, the stones are ancient and weather worn.

In the wall there is an equally old door, the wood is dark with age but stout and sturdy.

Now reach out your hand and push the door wide open.

Beyond you can see a beautiful garden.

The sun is shining and the garden looks fresh, green and inviting.

You step through the door and enter the world of the garden.

What do you see? Are there trees and flowers?

Is there a pathway? Is it broad and paved or just an earthen track?

Spend some time now exploring the garden.

(*pause*)

Now you are deep in the garden, turning a corner you come upon a beautiful sight.

Before you are two pools in each of which is a fountain, there is a path between and the spray from the fountains is causing a rainbow to form across the path.

As you go forward you walk through the damp air beneath the arch of the rainbow.

Ahead of you is a small summer house. What does it look like?

You approach the summer house and see there is someone inside with their head half turned away from you.

You feel a warm glow of recognition.

This other person is part of you, they are your Higher Self. Perhaps you may see this person as a Beloved Twin, or maybe a lover, they may be of the same or opposite sex as your physical self. In whatever form this person appears to you, they are someone very precious to you and dearly beloved.

You enter the summer house and greet your Beloved, now is the time for you to be together in the peace of this beautiful garden.

(*pause for meditation*)

As you leave the garden, you say your farewells and in your own time make your way back, under the rainbow and out through the old door in the garden wall, back to your present physical time and place.

When you have returned open your eyes and

acknowledge your presence in this room.

PART TWO
Before this meditation I want you to think of something which is a problem to you. This may be an aspect of your personality you want to change, something you regret and still carry a feeling of guilt about, some habit you wish to change or something you feel you compulsively do, such as smoking, and would like to stop doing. Whatever it may be take the thought of it into this meditation with you.
(relaxation and preparation for entering the inner worlds.)
You are standing before an old high wall, the stones are ancient and weather worn.

In the wall there is an equally old door, the wood is dark with age but stout and sturdy.

Now reach out your hand and push the door wide open.

Beyond you can see a beautiful garden.

You recognise the garden and you feel a rush of joy that you will soon meet your Higher Self once again.

Make your way through the garden, under the rainbow and go once more to the summer house.

Inside the summer house your Beloved is seated, enter and go to him/her.

Now I want you to share with your Beloved whatever it is you want to change, be completely honest about it, admit you cannot resolve this problem alone and ask for help.

Make a commitment to allow them to help you, ask for a symbol, a word or an image that you can bring to mind whenever you need their assistance in your everyday life when this problem arises.

Think of the people who you feel you have caused any harm or sorrow to through your actions.

Mentally tell them of your wish to change and set things right between you.

Ask your Beloved to help you to gain strength, through learning to contact that Source which is the Divine in the spiritual worlds.

Now spend a little time just being with your Beloved

Now it is time to return, when you are ready, say your farewells and in your own time make your way back through the garden, under the rainbow and out through the old door in the wall, and back to your present physical time and place.

When you have returned open your eyes and acknowledge your presence in this room.

The Search

You are going on a quest, a search for a place you know exists but which you have forgotten the path you must take to find it.

Perhaps you have been there in a dream or a meditation, you have an elusive memory of being very happy and at home there.

First of all you must prepare for the journey. Decide what you're wearing, do you wear a robe or just everyday clothes?

Are you wearing a hat? If so, does its shape and style have any particular meaning for you?

In your hand you are carrying a lamp. It can be electrical or have a living flame.

Before you is a doorway, it is surrounded by a heavy stone arch, the door is slightly ajar and you can see nothing beyond it.

Notice anything particular about the door, then push it open so that you can pass through.

You are glad of the light in your hand even though it only illuminates a small area of the way ahead.

You find yourself in a rock passageway, you touch the walls to see if they are wet or dry.

You walk forward down the passageway until at last there is a gleam of light ahead and you emerge into a large cave. There is plenty of light coming through openings in the roof and at the far side from the opening of the cave itself.

Suddenly you notice there is a seated figure blocking your way to the exit from the cave.

It is an ancient man, bearded and severe. Before him are two large books in which he is busily writing.

He looks up and notices you, then tells you that you cannot go further unless you answer his questions. You feel somewhat dismayed.

The old man tells you that only what is written in his books is the truth, that feelings and emotions are unreliable and only the facts and laws in his books are of value. Do you believe him?

He beckons you to look into his books. You go forward and look - what do you see?

Suddenly you realise that this old man cannot prevent you from going further, all you have to do is walk past him and continue. He turns round and calls after you, saying that you will regret not listening to him, but you smile and feel a little sorry for him, locked into his fixed and rigid thinking.

Journeys in the Light Within

As you come to the cave opening it is transformed into a beautiful carved archway, on either side are the carved figures of angels, their wings soaring upwards to meet at the high point of the arch. The sunlight streaming through the arch makes the figures glow and shine as if they were carved from light itself.

You step forward under their wings and emerge into the bright daylight.

Where are you? Look about you and remember this place so that you will be able to find the path when you wish to return.

There is a faint sweet sound just on the edge of hearing. It grows slowly louder yet remains elusive, you cannot quite decide where it is coming from.

Then around the corner of a tall rock you notice a small figure; it is the player of the melody.

Do you recognise him? What kind of instrument is he playing?

The small figure moves away and his tune calls to you with an irresistible desire to follow. Where does he lead you?

At last you find yourself beside a beautiful lake, the water is clear and calm and it is surrounded by tall trees. Swans make ripples across the still water as they swim across and now and then circles appear as fish leap and fall back into the water.

You follow the path around the lake enjoying the beauty and the warm sunlight.

Then, coming towards you down the path you see a couple, a man and a woman, mature and wise looking yet beautiful with a youthfulness about them. They smile at you and greet you.

You remain with them for what seems a long time,

gently talking and exchanging thoughts and ideas.

Then it is time to leave and they each hold out a hand to you, the woman smiles and tells you her name is Love, the man gives you his blessing and tells you his name is Harmony. They tell you to come and visit them whenever you feel the need to do so.

You walk on alongside the lake. Then the sunlight grows brighter, so bright the scene seems to be dissolving and disappearing.

All at once you notice there no longer seems to be a path beneath your feet and you are floating effortlessly as if in a sea of golden light.

Here you do not need wings to fly nor arms to swim, you just move in a sea of joy and light.

Allow yourself to be happy here and remember everything you experience.

At last you begin to feel yourself floating downwards, you feel the pull of the earth beneath you and slowly come to rest on solid ground.

As you feel your familiar body shape form about you once more notice if you feel different. How has this experience changed you?

Now you see that you are in a street of a small town, you see others about you and recognise them as your fellow travellers on this quest.

You are all walking in the same direction, then at the end of the street you see a stone archway and a familiar door.

You go through the door and find yourself once more back in the physical world.

Take a few moments to fully awaken to your physical body then open your eyes and acknowledge your presence here in this room.

Inner Cleansing

As you relax and close your eyes it seems you are slowly descending into a warm light mist that swirls about you in strange shapes and colours. You look into the formless veil and slowly a landscape takes shape around you.

You are standing on boggy ground, small pools of peaty water are dotted on the marshy land before you. In the distance rises a mountain range, at their foot the land is green and brown, as it rises it becomes grey, barren and forbidding. Clouds wreathe about the summits.

This is a bleak and unwelcoming place. A noise to your left makes you turn and you see a man winding his way towards you, he chooses his way carefully between the bog and pools. He is dressed in dark green trousers and matching over jacket made from thick material which is obviously designed to repel both the cold and the rain of this inhospitable place. Seeing you he draws a heavy and serviceable looking sword from its scabbard at his waist. In a deep and rather alarming voice he challenges you – "Who comes here". You answer in confident tones that you are a seeker come to the inner worlds seeking self-knowledge and cleansing. With a strange and secret smile he tells you that he is the Challenger whom all Seekers meet upon their Quest. To go further, he says, you must meet him face to face and acknowledge your own deficiencies and limitations of which he is but the reflection. He tells you that if you would go deeper into the worlds he guards you must be prepared to overcome all obstacles and face your own unconscious fears and self-limitations. Gathering your courage you tell him that you wish to go on and ask him to be your guide through the marsh lands and onto safer ground. He nods briefly then turns and stalks away.

You hurry to follow him not wanting to lose sight of him in the mist. You seem to walk for a long time over the marsh grass, twisting and turning as you avoid the pools which constantly appear in your path. And in each pool you see reflected your secret fears, prejudices, limitations, ignorance and the bondage you have set about your thinking.

As you pass each pool you see these old ideas sink deep into the depths of the water, become absorbed and then disappear.

Journeys in the Light Within

At last you feel firm ground beneath your feet, and you find yourself walking on a dark heathland. Your Guide still marches ahead of you and you have only time to glance briefly about as you hurry after him. This place is no more welcoming than was the marshland. All around are the signs of violent destruction as if recent warfare has swept over the land. A sudden flash of heat and light hits you and to your left you see a small building engulfed in savage flames. A pall of black smoke whips crazily in the wind and the orange red flames shoot into the troubled sky. Looking into the heart of the fire you see that while it is destructive it is also cleansing. In it you see small bundles which suddenly blaze into flame and are then consumed by the fire.

A wise knowing grows within you and you know the contents of the bundles. They are your own fears, the memories you would rather not acknowledge, the thwarted plans and unkind thoughts which lie deeply buried in us all. The fire takes them and cleanses them, you can let them go to be reborn in new and brighter thoughts and emotions.

Feeling lightened and cleansed you step out with renewed vigour. The landscape changes and you find yourself walking in a green meadow beside a quiet lake. Beside the shore is a castle, lights gleam invitingly from its windows and you hurry forward anticipating shelter and warmth. You approach the large wooden door and knock loudly upon it. Immediately it swings open and inside you see a large hall with rich furnishings and a huge log fire blazing at the far end. You hesitate waiting for someone to greet you - but there is only silence and the empty hall. The temptation to warm yourself at the fire is great and with a beating heart you enter the hall, closing the door gently behind you.

You look around at the ornate furnishings, low comfortable looking leather chairs, carved cabinets and thick carpets on the floor. You walk over to the fire, then hearing a slight noise, you turn to see a girl in a long green robe watching you. She smiles slightly, and beckons you to follow her through a door at the rear of the hall. Thinking that at last you will meet the owners of the castle you follow. But it is a will o' the wisp tour of the castle on which you have embarked. Just as you enter a room you see a glimpse of the green dress disappear around another doorway. Then strange things begin to happen.

You reach for a doorknob - and the door vanishes. You try to pick up a candle - and touch empty air. You think you see the girl smiling invitingly at you and it is your own reflection in a window. At last you come into a room where there is an appetising meal laid out on a richly prepared table. You touch a piece of fruit and the whole table dissolves into a shimmer of colour. Your nerves are stretched tight and you doubt the reality of everything here. Then a door opens in front of you, you step through and find yourself in a kind of audience chamber.

At the far end of the hall is a seated figure. He wears a long robe of some heavy white material and a rich, fur trimmed, scarlet cloak, upon his brow is a circlet of gold and in his hand the symbol of his sovereignty. He beckons you to approach and you do so with trepidation, expecting him to disappear at any moment. But he does not. As you come nearer you see he is a man of mature years yet still with youthful vigour. As though he knows your thoughts, he tells you that he is the first true image you have seen since you entered the castle. This is the place of self-deception and illusion, here you meet all your own false fantasies, are dazzled by glamour and see the results of un-controlled emotions. Turning slightly he points to the wall on your left hand. You turn also and see there an archway in the stone wall of the castle. Beyond there is a brilliant light which seems to be coming from a strange and ornate cross behind a small altar on which burn two long white candles. The cross could be carved from stone, but then again it has almost the human shape of a man stood with arms outstretched, and surely you see a calm and serene face where the loop of the cross should be? A feeling of awe sweeps over you and you feel a great urge to approach and pay homage to these sacred symbols which seem to embody all the goals of your quest.

Then just as you are about to rush forward the image crumbles and slowly disintegrates and falls to the ground in a thousand pieces. The shock makes your senses reel and you feel a deep sense of loss and disbelief. "Put not your trust in images" says the voice of the man upon the throne. "Such things dazzle unless they are your own creations made from your own experience. Look to the Light which dwells in your own heart, seek Truth, and give Love. Thus will you follow always your own star." Feeling somewhat foolish at his perception of all these hidden facets of your character you long to turn away and regain your lost composure. He smiles, somewhat sympathetically, then tells you that in gaining this self-knowledge you

Journeys in the Light Within

have already broken the spell of the castle of illusion. As he says this he extends his hand in blessing towards you and slowly fades from view.

For a time you see only the bare stones of the castle wall then an image starts to form. At first just a hint of colour which slowly solidifies into the figure of a beautiful woman, tall and slender. Her deep purple robe falls in heavy folds to her feet and from her shoulders hangs a cloak of forest green. Upon her brow a diadem of gold with the Star of Wisdom shining brilliantly from its centre. You catch your breath at her beauty and feel the love and compassion which radiates from her. For a moment you hesitate, not wishing to fall once more into the illusionary world of the castle, but the woman smiles and by the love which she emanates draws you towards her. In her hands is a golden chalice filled to the brim with clear crystal water. This is the water of self- knowledge, she holds out the chalice bids you drink. As you do so you feel new strength and confidence flood into you and you feel the Light of your own Star pulsing gently within you. As the Lady stands aside you see a doorway open in the wall behind her. The land beyond is bathed in moonlight and in the night sky the stars shine with glittering intensity.

You walk through the doorway into the night air and find yourself on a plateau overlooking the sea. The castle is no longer there but in its place is a circle of ancient stones with a great fire burning in its centre. The fire draws you and you pass between the stones and enter the circle. You notice a figure seated by the fire. He is old yet young, his warm robe is the brown of the Earth and about him are gathered the children of the Earth. A rabbit nestles in the fold of his robe, a swallow sits upon his shoulder, a great stag guards his back and all about him are the small creatures of land and forest. He extends a hand in welcome and bids you join the circle. Now are you caught up in song and story as he sings and recites tales of ancient times and future visions. He tells of the old heroes of this land, of battles fought and won for freedoms sake. Of sages who brought wisdom and the Bright Bearers of the Light he speaks. Then stretching out his hand he places a golden thread across your palm and with it weaves a link between us all. Smiling he tells you that by its aid you will always be able to find your way back to his sacred fire and by its warmth and light learn wisdom for yourself. Here you can touch inspiration and insight, learn spiritual truths and, in due time, open the inner doorways which are initiation in the Light in the reality of the inner worlds. You sit quietly for a time, just taking in all the quietude and peace of this time and place.

Then a drowsiness creeps over you, your head drops slowly and you almost sleep. Rousing yourself you open your eyes, but all you can see is a light mist which swirls and wreathes about you then slowly clears and you find yourself back in your physical body and material reality.

The Seeker

As you relax and close your eyes you begin to let go of your outer self. Let the body settle into a comfortable posture and begin to focus your attention on the thoughts and images which arise as you go deeper into our inner self.

You are standing on a grassy cliff top looking down into a wide deep valley. Beside you is a small tree with dark evergreen like leaves. It is the only thing, apart from the grass, which appears to be living in this strange landscape. Far below you is a wide valley, a broad river twists its way down in large looping meanders. To your right are high mountains, snow clad and desolate, with steep escarpments and craggy peaks. As you stand looking around a hazy shimmer below catches your attention and you notice a beautiful rainbow which seems to start at your feet and curve downwards to the valley floor.

In this inner world you are not bound by the laws of the physical world, you step out onto the rainbow, knowing that you are quite safe and could fly if you so wished. It is a strange sensation to see nothing but the bands of colour beneath your feet and the valley floor far below. The sensation is exhilarating and with a laugh of pure pleasure you start to run down the rainbow, faster and faster you go until you are almost sliding - then with a slight jolt you land in the valley and look back to see the little green tree far above you.

The mountains look even larger and bleaker from here, and you are wondering if coming down the rainbow was a good idea when you are hailed by a figure standing at the edge of the river. The man is tall and has a great mass of bright red hair which curls and springs in unruly coils about his head. He wears a band across his forehead which is obviously designed to control it but with little success. He is dressed in thick woollen trousers and a bright yellow shirt. Over all of this he is wearing a very serviceable looking chain mail shirt. In his right hand he holds a sword and in his left a shield on which is emblazoned a magical pentacle. He challenges you and asks your purpose in this land. You reply that you have come seeking experience of the inner worlds and to add to your knowledge. He nods briefly as if this answer at least partially satisfies him.

Then he tells you that he is the champion of the Lady who rules this land and that, if you truly wish to learn, it is to her that you should be travelling. You hastily assure him that you do indeed wish to learn and ask him if he will show you the way to the Lady.

After another long and very searching look into your eyes he nods briefly then turns and walks briskly away. It seems you have not been refused, even if you are not especially invited, to follow him. So you make haste to do so and soon find yourself standing just behind our Guide on the bank of the river. Here it has become deep and fast flowing, and you feel some apprehension at the thought of where he may be leading you. Walking swiftly along the riverbank you turn round a bend and there before you is a large rowing boat. It has sails but they are tightly furled against the mast. Your Guide indicates that you should board the boat and taking your courage in both hands you climb over the steep side and seat yourself on the hard, wooden bench which is the only seating the boat offers. Then as if rowed by unseen hands the boat sets sail into the middle of the river and you are tossed and thrown as it is caught by the strong current.

The river plunges into a steep sided gully and the cliffs loom so close you are full of fear that you will crash against the dark rock. But then in a small corner of your mind you remember that this is the inner world and no physical harm can come to you. It is only your own fear which can frighten you. The thought gives you courage and you begin to enjoy the wild ride down the tossing heaving river. The waves crash on the side of the boat and their white tops form strange shapes which you can almost imagine are the living forms of weird river creatures long vanished from your own world.

This wild journey tests your courage and determination to the utmost. You know you can stop the journey any time you wish but the will to go on is stronger than your fear. At last the waters quieten and flow into a broad valley. The unseen oarsmen bring it to a gentle mooring and with relief you climb out of the boat onto a small sandy beach. Beyond the beach are tall and ancient trees whose golden leaves dance in the light breeze and allow the sunlight to filter through to the floor of the wood which is golden and russet with the autumn leaves.

Your Guide strides to the edge of the wood and stands as if listening. You strain your ears trying to pick up any sound but there is only the soft rush of the wind in the trees and the distant roar of the river. You become aware of a new faint melodious sound, gradually getting louder and louder, the sound of a harp being most beautifully played. The harpist appears through the trees, a gentle looking man astride a white horse, playing as he rides. He smiles when he sees you and exchanges a quiet greeting with your Guide who explains your presence and asks that you be taken further on your Quest to meet the Lady. With a brief nod the Harpist indicates his willingness to help and with a small wave of his hand in your direction he turns and rides slowly back into the wood.

You follow and to your surprise you easily keep pace. The wood is quite beautiful and never becomes so dense that you feel oppressed. The sunlight filters through the trees and is warm and comforting after the cold river. The Rider turns from time to time to make certain you are still following and gives you a shy smile of encouragement and companionship. You are enjoying the walk so much that you hardly notice the time passing until you arrive in a clearing. Before you is a very sturdy house built of natural stone, grass grows from its roof and it seems to be just another part of the wood. The doorway is formed of two great stone pillars supporting a massive stone lintel. You hesitate, wondering if you are expected to enter. The Harpist does not pause in his song and as if in response to his melody The Lady comes from the house.

    She is tall and graceful in her movements. Her long gown reaches to her ankles and there are soft moccasins upon her feet. On her wrist sits a hawk which spreads its wings at sight of us, then settles back to rest at a quiet word from the Lady. She is Linnet, Lady of the Woods, she asks what you seek. You explain once more that you are seeking new knowledge and experience in the inner worlds. She smiles and says that she will give you some insight into the ways of the woods, its animals and the creatures who dwell there. Before you can say your thanks she is gone and only the Hawk remains hovering in the air.

    You feel a strange sensation as you realise that you too are hovering in the air and when you try to lift your arms you find they are now wings and the motion has lifted you high into the sky. Up and up you go following the Hawk, soon you are looking down on the treetops and can see the mountains far away on the horizon. The view is breath taking and so beautiful. You climb yet higher, you are caught by the currents in the air, you twist and turn helplessly. With a flick of the wing you are stabilised and you have mastered this new way of travelling. You rise and fall on the hidden air waves, you swoop and dive almost back to earth, then soar again high into the clouds. Now you understand what it feels like to be able to fly and your usual earth-bound travel seems so limiting. For a long time you enjoy this freedom of flight, then the Hawk gives a loud call and you know you must follow him back to earth. Down and down you go, straight through a gap in the treetops and into a glade surrounded by tall pine trees. In the centre of the clearing is a large bolder on which the Hawk rests, you gently land next to him. Then, in an instant, he is gone and the lady Linnet sits upon the stone. She smiles at your surprise and laughs outright at the spectacle you make, half bird, half human. Another clap of her hands and you are back in your familiar human shape once more.

    The Lady Linnet starts to sing softly, her voice is gentle as a summer breeze, it rises and falls like the sound of the sighing trees and holds you totally spellbound. Then the creatures of the forest come, creeping from the trees and settling at her feet. Small animals, weasels and rabbits, mice and moles peep out from the borders of her skirts. Then forming a ring about you are the majestic stag, a pack of wolves, a large, powerful bear and the wild hog, all listening to the Lady's song and totally ignoring your presence.

    Slowly the circle grows as wild cats, deer, and even sheep and other domestic creatures come to pay homage at the Lady's call. A realisation slowly dawns in your consciousness as you realise that you too are but another creature of the wood. Those about you share the same needs and respond to the same calls from deep within their nature. You are not separate from the stream of life which flows upon this planet but part of the manifestation of the Eternal in all its myriad forms. A great wave of understanding floods over you and you know the individuality behind each pair of eyes, be they those of creatures large or small, animal or human.

Then you feel the eyes of the Lady fixed upon you, she smiles and in unspoken communication tells you that you have received that for which you came. Then as you watch the Lady vanishes and in her place the Hawk sits once more upon the stone. With lazy wings he rises slowly into the air and you find yourself flying once more upwards into the clear sky. The mountains rise into view and you follow the Hawk as he climbs towards them. Then below you see the cliff top from where your journey started and the little tree which grows upon it. You feel yourself floating irresistibly downwards, landing beside the Tree. Reaching out a hand you see that you are back into your own familiar form. The mountains fade from view, you become aware once more of the material world and find yourself seated in the room where you started your journey. Back in your own place and time on Earth but also bringing with you a new understanding of your world and its inhabitants.

Wisdom, Strength and Beauty

You are going upon a journey, a journey which is both an adventure and a quest. Physically you are going nowhere, but in the realm of the mind there are no restrictions of space and distance. You are also not limited by time as you are in the material world, your adventure can be as brief or lengthy in real time as you wish.

You allow yourself to relax and focus your attention into the inner world. Before you forms a light mist which swirls gently as if drifting in a light breeze. As you walk forward into the mist it thins and then clears completely. You look about to see where your adventure is to start and find you are standing on a deserted quay in a small harbour. Below the water of the harbour rises and falls in the gentle rhythm of an incoming tide which is almost at the full. Moored to the side of the quay is a strange looking boat. Like a large wooden rowing boat with steeper sides and a brow which curves upwards and backwards towards the inside and which is carved into the shape of a strange mythical animal. There are no rowers but the boat has a single large rectangular sail hanging from a crossbeam, balanced at the bottom by an equally long beam. From the top of the central mast stretch two long chains, one to each end of the boat. On the sail are strange symbols which you vaguely recognise.

There is nobody in sight to direct you so after a little hesitation you obey your strong impulse to board the boat. It sways under your weight and you quickly sit down on the wooden seats to restore its stability.

With a slightly uneasy feeling you notice that the boat is no longer stationary but gliding slowly towards the harbour entrance. In a short time it is out on the open sea and the swell of the boat increases, but not unpleasantly. The boat behaves as if guided by an unseen crew and steers a course southward following the coastline which is visible through a mist rising several feet over the sea. Above the mist you can see a range of mountains with summits darkly etched against the brightly lit clouds.

You sail for some time before realising that the coastline has disappeared and there is only the silver

Journeys in the Light Within

sea stretching out in all directions. You feel a little alarmed at the isolation but before you can become overly concerned you notice the tall cliffs of a coastline ahead. The sea crashes against the grey rocks of the cliffs and all you can see of the land is rolling green heath stretching away into the distance. There is no sign of any habitation or harbour. Your strange craft continues to move forward with certainty and purpose and just as you fear it will crash against the rocks, you notice a small inlet directly ahead. The boat, with faultless certainty, enters. The cliffs tower above as the inlet takes a curving course between them. The steep sides of the inlet fall away abruptly and you sail out onto a large lake surrounded on all sides by a series of green hills. The boat continues its course across the waters of the lake and finally comes to rest against a small wooden jetty. With some relief you stand up and step out of the boat, glad to stretch your legs after the long sail.

As you reach the shore you see a well-trodden path leading away from the beach, it seems natural to follow it. It is pleasant walking over the springy grass, the sun warming you after the cool breeze of the sea voyage.

You come upon a river crossing the path and the only way ahead is by a small wooden footbridge. To your horror the way is barred by a very large, ferocious looking brown bear, his lips go back in a snarl and a deep growl comes from his very depths. If you go back you can't be certain the boat will be waiting for you, if you go forward you have to pass the bear to cross the bridge. As indecision holds you immobile and fear ripples down your spine you notice that all is not well with the bear, one of its feet is locked in a cruel looking trap. Your heart goes out in pity and gathering all your courage you slowly walk nearer. The bear growls again deep in its throat, you hesitate before speaking to it, quietly and reassuringly. As if it begins to sense your friendly intention the growls subside, and slowly you move nearer – without warning a paw shoots out and knocks you off balance. Your heart leaps in alarm and the though crosses your mind that you will leave the bear to its fate, but one look at the trapped foot and compassion stirs your heart.

With more gentle murmurs and soft words you again advance. This time the bear allows your approach and with a fast beating heart you reach out towards the trap. He sits quietly which reassures you as you put both hands on the mechanism and begin to force the trap open. As the jaws come fully open and the leg is free a mighty screaming cry blasts your ears, the bear flings its newly released paw high above you - and you wait for the blow. For an instant of frozen horror and fear your world stops - but the bear is no longer there and, in its stead, a young and shining warrior stands before you. Instead of an upraised paw poised to strike you down, a gleaming sword is held above your head. The young man smiles at your consternation then touches you lightly upon the head with his sword. "So have you proved your courage and compassion" he says. "Mine is the strength of the warrior who fights for all who need protection and succour, my strength you have made your own." Thus saying he steps towards you and like two images sliding into one he blends with you, then you feel his power and strength become part of yourself.

Feeling somewhat shaken you cross the bridge and walk on upon the path which follows the far side of the river through a gentle green meadow. You enjoy the peace of this place and soon feel ready for further adventure.

The path takes you into a wood of silver birch trees where the ground is covered with ferns and small low growing shrubs. The sunlight dances through the leaves and the river flows gently along beside you. The peace and serenity of the place are so beguiling you are rendered totally unprepared when rounding a bend you almost fall over a bundle of old rags lying across the path. The bundle starts to move, and a harsh rending groan hits your ears. As you bend down to look closer, horror sweeps over you at the sight of an ancient woman lying amid the rags, hair matted, her skin covered with sores and over all evidence of neglect and sickness. The woman groans again and looking up into your eyes she feebly stretches out one hand towards you and whispers "water." Everything within you recoils from touching her - and yet you cannot in humanity refuse her request. Beside her lies a dirty earthenware cup. You pick it up and go down to the riverbank and clean it as best you can in the sweet fresh water. Then filling it you return to the old woman. Swallowing hard to suppress your revulsion you place one hand behind her filthy head to lift it high enough for her to drink. She sips the water - and disappears. You look up in consternation, to meet the most beautiful pair of eyes you have ever seen smiling down into your own.

Their owner is tall and graceful, her soft green gown clinging to the curves of her perfect figure. She reaches out a slender hand to take the cup which you are still holding and it is changed to a gleaming golden chalice filled to the brim with sparkling fresh water. The Lady takes the chalice from your trembling hands and says, "So have you proved your humanity and your love. Mine is the beauty and truth of nature and the land. Through me you will see the beauty in all things and the unity of all that lives." She holds out the chalice towards you and bids you drink. The water is sweet and cool and as it flows into you, so too, it seems does the Lady, you feel her grace and beauty become part of you in some deep and mysterious way. When you look up you are once more alone - and yet you look with new eyes and a deeper understanding at the beauty of the forest about you. Refreshed and invigorated you continue your walk along the path. You are no longer alone, small creatures dart out from the undergrowth and dance unafraid across your path. A deer raises its proud head to stare at you and about your heads the birds and insects dance in a kaleidoscope of colour. You are one with nature.

Deeper and deeper into the forest the path takes you. The trees become more varied and dense. The path is covered with pine needles and dry, russet coloured leaves which rustle and crunch beneath your feet. The top of the trees are high above your head and only the occasional sunbeam manages to find its way to the forest floor. Just ahead you see a bright light, it is a small clearing with the sun flooding in. You feel the sun's warmth as you emerge from the shadow of the trees.

The clearing is no accident of nature for it is obvious the trees have been cleared purposely. You notice a small round hut with a thatched type roof just across from where you stand, a heavy woollen curtain hangs across the entrance and a thin column of light grey smoke curls upwards from the top of the roof. You are irresistibly drawn to it and find yourself standing at the curtained doorway. A brusque voice, apparently from nowhere, says "Well come in then", it startles you. Too stunned to do otherwise you draw aside the curtain step within. For a few moments you can see nothing after the bright sunlight, then as your eyes become accustomed to the low light you see first a small fire of dry tree branches, the grey smoke curls upwards and disappears through the hole in the roof. "Sit down then", you jump at the sharp command and hurriedly obey. Now you see more clearly you perceive the figure of a man dressed in a long brown woollen gown seated against the wall of the hut. He is watching you with penetrating eyes and an uninviting expression. He asks if you know where the path you are following is leading. You explain that you have gained much in following it thus far and feel sure it will eventually lead you to even higher experiences. He smiles slightly as if amused by your trust and enthusiasm. Your heart sinks a little at this lack of encouragement and you feel your confidence in your adventure slipping away. As if he knows your hidden doubts and misgivings he begins to enlarge upon all the dangers and difficulties you will encounter if you persist, dampening your spirits. Then, you notice the fire, its warmth reaches out to touch you and the flames seem to grow brighter as if speaking of hope and promise instead of gloom and despair.

Looking into the fire you remember that it is always light which beckons you onwards and you turn with renewed confidence to face the man. You tell him the light within you, which has brought you this far, will surely be your guide and protection. The living fire which is your life energy blazes upwards through your body and the light of your spirits hope shines steadily at the centre of your being. You look back into his eyes, your own are now filled with confidence and knowledge. His stern eyes begin to soften and from their depths a smile of satisfaction grows until his whole face is transformed into one of joy and pleasure. Slowly rising he comes to stand before you and in his hands is a large book with closely written pages. He holds the book towards you and bids you take it saying: "this book which I give you contains all that you have learnt till now on all your journeys, take it and use it well. The book is not yet complete and there are pages for you still to write upon, see that you fill it well. My gift to you is access to my thoughts for I am near you always, my name is Wisdom."

With trembling hands you take the book and hold it close, it enters you and settles in your heart.

All is still and quiet about you and you rest in this deep tranquillity for some time. When at last you stir you know you must once more return to your own world and put the gifts to good and useful purpose. Rising to your feet you leave the hut and once more find the path. As you walk the whole forest seems to join in your pleasure and rejoicing, the wind sings in the treetops, the sunlight dances across the ground and all the birds, animals and plants seem to fly and run and grow with an added zest.

At last the trees come to an end and you are standing on rising ground overlooking a fair and fertile plain and, in the distance, the shining surface of the sea. You begin to descend with anxious eyes scanning the water for your boat. Coming towards you up the path you see a fair, young maiden who waves in greeting and signs for you to follow her. Grateful for a guide at last you make haste to catch up, yet the faster you walk the more she seems to keep just beyond your reach but never quite going out of sight. So intent are you with keeping her in view you have not noticed how far you have travelled and are surprised to find yourself back on the shore with your boat riding gently at anchor near the little jetty. Your guide indicates that you should board, and when you are once more safely seated she bids you farewell telling you to care well for those things you take with you - the strength of the bear, the beauty of the Lady and the gift of Wisdom.

Sleepy now from your long adventure you doze with the gentle rhythm of the boat as it takes you back to your own place and time.

When you feel the boat bump against the harbour wall you know you have returned. Climbing from the boat you walk towards the land, soon you are enveloped in a light mist which swirls gently around, as it clears you find yourself back in your body. Back within your space and time and back in this room where you started your adventure.

The Pleiades

You are standing on a small headland, below you the sea gleams in the last afterglow of twilight. Above your head shines the vast panorama of the Universe against the dark velvet back cloth of the night sky.

It is full tide and the gently swelling sea breaks in a line of silver surf on the shingle beach below.

To your right the coastline sweeps away in a perfect bay which ends with another, far larger, headland away to the north.

There is a village nestling against the cliffs of the headland with a small harbour. Nets and lobster pots are neatly set out on the top of the harbour wall and a few boats ride at anchor, their lighted lanterns indicating that it will not be long before they too set sail for the nights work.

It is early summer and the light breeze is pleasant and refreshing. You begin to walk down from the headland through the bracken and short springy grass. You are almost down when, round the headland, comes a sight which brings you to a halt in sheer surprise and admiration. Gliding over the tranquil water, as if pulled by unseen hands, is a large galleon in full sail, shining with a silvery phosphorescent glow. As you watch it turns towards the harbour and you hurry onwards hoping to be able to obtain a closer view if it does indeed come to shore.

As you arrive on the quayside the galleon is coming through the harbour entrance. You watch as it sails towards you and then slowly turns sideways to dock against the harbour wall. From nowhere, willing helpers catch the ropes and soon the ship is safely secured and a gangway lowered to the land.

A small crowd has gathered to stare at the galleon in wonder and curiosity, you too are drawn towards it and become part of the group of silent watching people. For a little while nothing happens, then a solitary figure appears on the deck of the ship, dressed in a robe of dark, rough material, with the hood pulled well forward, the figure moves silently to the top of the gangway and stands looking down at the crowd below. With one swift movement the hood is pulled back to reveal a man of mature middle years, his grey head matched by a short, neatly trimmed, beard.

For a few moments he regards us in silence, then walks part way down the gangway before pausing once more. His voice, when he speaks, is sudden and unexpected , your heart give a slight leap of alarm. "Will you sail with me?" he says. A dozen questions race through your mind - where to? - why? - is it safe? Who is he? "If you fear do not come" the man says. Feeling a little foolish you look at the others with an unspoken question in your eyes. Then as one we all turn and walk towards the ship. The man smiles as if to himself, then turns and walks back onto the deck.

We climb the gangway and find ourselves on the curving planks of the galleon's deck, the sails making a soft rhythmic noise above us as they move in the slight breeze.

Once we are all aboard the silent crew reappear and set about their tasks making ready to sail. Before we realise it, we have left the harbour wall and the ship is turning and facing out to the open ocean. Soon the little town and the headland are far behind us and we are sailing out on the dark surface of the sea.

The robed man returns and beckons us to gather about him. He tells us that we are aboard a ship which sails on the deep seas of the mind, the ocean which looks so real does not restrict us as would the waters of our physical world. He explains that we are setting out on a voyage of discovery into the deep and mysterious realities of our own inner world. Declaring that there is nothing we need fear on this journey he asks us to relax and learn all we can from the experience.

Our first endeavour, he says, is to climb the seven rungs of the sacred ladder to the stars.

We crowd to the prow of the ship, the better to see where this strange journey will take us. The silver sea

Journeys in the Light Within

stretches before us to the far horizon then from behind a bank of low, dense clouds a brilliant full Moon slides into view, shining low on the horizon and making a pathway of light across the sea to the ship. Sailing down this shimmering highway, the ship sails on over the horizon towards the Moon. Below us now is only the velvet darkness of deep space and ahead is the ever-growing disc of the Moon. Nearer and nearer we sail until we are enveloped in its atmosphere.

Strange and powerful emotions begin to stir within you, you are caught up in a dream like world where your emotions are displayed in a series of swiftly changing images. You see yourself in a thousand different guises and in the seeing you understand the nature of your own hidden impulses. Strangely the vision gives you strength and a new sense of security.

The galleon sails on and soon we are out beyond the Moon's influence and have passed the first rung of the ladder.

On and on we sail, deeper and deeper into space, until we come into the influence of Venus, the second rung of the ladder. Here you dream of those you love and of the pleasures and richness of your Earth life, you see where you have failed to understand the needs of others and know how you have allowed the petty details of your lives to blind you to the wonders of your world. An icicle of uncaring melts within you as you accept the gift of enjoyment and pleasure which Venus radiates. Then we sail on.

A pulse of energy throbbing through your veins alerts you to the influence of the next rung of the ladder, the sphere of Mercury which energises and invigorates your mind. Here you receive the gift of intellect and a realisation of the capacity of humanity to climb to ever greater heights of achievement on the stored knowledge of our race.

Now before us shines the central sun of our solar system. Majestic, brilliant, awesome. So huge does it seem that you feel our little ship must be drawn into its fire and we too will be destroyed within it. But it is not so, for here you feel - not its heat, but the wisdom and the power of the Divinity which it is, the mighty symbol. As you pass through the fourth rung of the ladder you touch the essence of spirituality in your nature and you know that now it will forever be a conscious part of you, as it has always been. As you pass the closest point to the sun you bow your head, not only because the light is too bright for you to bear but also in reverence and worship of this great parent of your planet and your being.

As the vision of the sun recedes behind you, the ship sails on, ever deeper into space.

Then in the distance you see the red glow of the planet Mars and know you are about to pass through the fifth rung of the ladder. This time the ship passes nearer to the planet and you can see its colour quite plainly, with the strange marks upon its surface, which look so like constructed canals you wonder if indeed Mars has known life. You feel the overwhelming drive to action which is the force of this sphere, restless yet full of strength and vigour, a feeling that there is nothing which you could not tackle and conquer. Your Mentor reminds you gently not to get too carried away with this feeling lest you be tempted to use this force to inflict your will on others. The reminder is timely and you are still

Journeys in the Light Within

pondering on all the implications of the Mars force when you see the mighty planet Jupiter ahead of you.

As you approach, its influence flows towards you, bringing feelings of confidence and energy. You remember the warning about Mars and realise it would be easy for these feelings to become bravado and rash action if you let them have too much freedom. There is also a feeling of certain lightness of heart and joyousness in living.

At last, you reach the sphere of the seventh rung of the ladder, there before you is Saturn, spinning in space, its rings like diamond jewels enhancing its beauty. The feeling it brings is sobering and makes you aware that all the influences of the ladder are a part of your nature and that it is your responsibility to use them wisely and well.

Yur ship turns and for a moment you can look back and see all the planets spinning in their orbits around the Sun, our own Earth is home but also just another globe floating in space.

You feel a pull, which calls you home but your journey is not yet done. The ship sails on.

Now you have left our solar system far behind. Ahead of you the three great stars of Orion's Belt stretch across the sky and mighty Sirius rivals our own sun in size and brilliance.

Then from the deep dark sky behind Orion's Belt shines out the silver light of a family of stars. Close clustered in the sky the Sacred Pleiades welcomes our ship home.

In dark and distant ages their midnight culmination marked the year, on this night too it is said that great Atlantis fell. In every continent and every time they marked the seasons and the reign of Kings. Goddesses and Gods kept holy days at their rising and their sacred mysteries brought blessings and gifts to Earth.

Like seven doves they swoop down through the sky, as if to bring you messages of peace. Yet as they come it seems they shift and change and riding on the back of Taurus come seven maidens, fair in form and face. Six are fair in colouring and dress, their blonde hair and flowing white gowns streaming out behind them as they ride. But the seventh maiden is dark as ebony and her black gown deep and shining like liquid jet. Our Mentor holds out his arms in greeting as they circle the ship. Then one by one they alight on the deck.

Our Mentor explains that they bring you gifts to take with you back to Earth and bids you come forward in turn to receive them. Dazzled by the majestic beauty of the maidens we hesitate, but then one by one we go forward. Each maiden in turn places her hand upon our heads and names her gift.

The first gives understanding, the second gives sympathy, the third gives intuition, the fourth gives the power to listen, the fifth gives courage and the sixth gives you the knowledge of the continuity of life. But the dark seventh maiden places her hands on either side of our face and looks deeply into our eyes and from her we receive the gift of dreams.

No sooner are the gifts given than the maidens are gone and all that we can see of them is seven birds which circle the ship once and fly swiftly away and are lost in the darkness.

The stars about you wheel and change and you

realise that the ship has changed direction and far in the distance you can once more see our own sun and its family of planets. You feel the ship increase its speed and soon we have passed the path of Saturn and watch the other planets pass you by as we sail unerringly towards the seas of Earth. Before you know it you are on the Moon path and once more on an earthly ocean.

The wind blows cool but strong and the galleon sails true. Soon you see a familiar coastline and a small harbour entrance. The crew have brought you safely back to the harbour and very quickly they have the ship tied safely and secure.

Our Mentor tells you that it is time for you to part and for him to continue his voyage through the Universe. He gives each one of you his blessing as we leave the ship. We walk down the gangway and gather in a silent group and say goodbye. No sooner are we ashore than the galleon is once more setting sail, you watch it for a long time until it disappears from view into the far distance. Then you turn and begin your walk back to the headland and the unseen but familiar doorway which leads you back into your own physical world.

The Castle of the Shore

As you relax and close your eyes you begin to see a filmy mist forming before your eyes. Let yourself drift into the mist and as you do so let your body become fully relaxed and at ease. This is a time of relaxation and rest for the body so let it sink almost into a light sleep, but at the same time keep your inner awareness very much awake.

Look into the mist and watch it swirl in front of you as if blown by a light breeze. The breeze begins to blow gently on your face and you become aware that you are standing on a seashore.

The sand is soft and golden beneath your feet, and you see the wide sweep of a beautiful bay curving away to your right. Behind the bay are high sand dunes where sharp bladed grass bends and dances in the soft wind.

The dunes shield the bay from your view of the land and you cannot guess where this shore may be. Before you the wide blue expanse of the sea with small white capped waves ripples swiftly in to wash gently at your feet. To your left the coast becomes rocky and tall cliffs rise sharply, their reddish coloured stone warm in the pale sunlight.

You notice a small island rising steeply from the sea some mile out from the shore, half masked in a light mist which makes it seem to appear and disappear as you watch. A gap appears in the mist giving you a clearer view and you realise that what at first you thought were rocks and cliffs are in fact the high walls and pinnacles of a castle seeming to grow from the rock itself. Indeed, it seems more as if the Castle were carved of the living rock than that a building had been constructed from it.

So enchanted are you by this sight that you do not notice that the tide is slowly receding and now there is an expanse of wet sand between you and the sea. Rocks and seaweed are revealed in scattered patterns as the water leaves them high and dry upon the shore. You notice one area of sand has a more regular flat appearance than the rest and you walk forward to see why. Before your startled eyes a pathway is revealed which leads straight into the waters of the sea, you trace its path until it fades from view as the water deepens. For a moment you are totally puzzled by the sight before realising that the path is going in the direction of the Castle and the prospect of being able to reach the castle fills you with a deep excitement. With total fascination you stand and watch the tide go out and gradually more of the pathway is revealed. Soon it becomes obvious that the path is raised above the level of the sand, a causeway wide enough for a car slowly comes into view.

Looking up towards the Castle you sense a deep longing to stand within its walls. You walk forward and take the first few steps on the pathway, to your surprise the water has left the surface clean, firm and secure to walk upon.

You walk out further and further along the causeway, the sea still flowing on either side. The water is shallow and clear, and you see small fish darting quickly among the waves and seaweed gently swaying to the rhythm of the tide. Parts of the path are still covered by the water and occasionally you have to pause and wait until it is passable.

At last the way is clear and you can see the last few yards of the path beneath the sea. You walk forward enjoying the feel of the cool water washing over your feet and, in the last few yards, rising high to your knees. You feel the path begin to rise slightly and in a few moments you are on dry land.

So engrossed have you been in watching the path that you had not noticed the Castle drawing near. You raise your eyes and it is there. Steep cliffs rise above your head and the rampart walls surmount them some thirty feet above you. The path now rises steeply and you see before you a tall graceful archway. There are no gates and you walk straight through into a large square courtyard.

The sides of the courtyard are formed by the fronts

Journeys in the Light Within

of buildings which look as if they may be offices or large halls. They are built of stone of the same colour and texture as the rock upon which the Castle stands so the effect is as if they were also part of it.

Crossing the courtyard you come to another, but smaller, archway. You find your way barred by a heavy wooden doorway. From the stone pillar of the archway hangs a large shining bell, it seems natural to just grasp the rope which hangs from it and ring the bell. The sudden sharp sound startles you as it seems to echo back and forth around the Castle. In some trepidation you wait for a response.

A sudden creak makes you look towards the door, you notice a small opening has appeared and realise you are being assessed by someone within. The door opens slowly to reveal the slender figure of a young girl in a long white robe who smiles at you shyly. She bids you welcome and gently taking your hand draws you through the doorway into the inner courtyard

Following the girl you pass through a series of passages and rooms and are surprised that the castle is so spacious. Eventually you come into a large, airy room whose tall windows look straight out over the sea. The room is spacious and comfortably furnished and there is an impression of warmth and tranquillity.

The girl indicates that you should go forward into the room alone. You walk towards the windows and notice a tall backed chair and seated in it is a man who is watching you with an intent gaze. He is neither old nor young but has an air of vigour and vitality about him. Inclining his head slightly in greeting he indicates that you should be seated in a low chair close beside him. He bids you welcome to the Castle of the Shore and ask what brings you there. You explain that you saw the Castle from the mainland and felt a strange and compelling urge to visit. He smiles as if he knows exactly what you mean and explains that the castle is a very special place and while it has a physical plane reality it also is a very real place upon the more subtle planes of existence, somewhere people come to contact those who dwell more deeply in the Inner Light. He tells you that the efforts you have made towards the development of your inner self have made it possible for you to have access to the castle and that it is your own inner need which has enabled you to discover it. You feel a deep thrill of excitement and anticipation and wait eagerly for him to continue. He says that you may just sit and talk to him, discuss any problems or questions you might have. You think for a time and say you would very much like to be able to do this and ask if you may return in the future for another visit. He smiles and tells you that you may come back any time you feel the need to do so. You sit and talk for a while and he gives you wise council and advice. As he indicates that your time with him is drawing to a close he asks if you would like to visit the chapel of the castle before you leave. You accept with eager anticipation and as if she has been summoned the young girl returns to the room. The man smiles at you and touches your forehead in blessing before bidding you farewell.

You turn and follow the girl who leads you once more through the passageways and halls of the Castle emerging at last onto a grassed area overlooking the sea. To your left you can just see the cliffs of the mainland and part of the bay and ahead of you stands

Journeys in the Light Within

the chapel. She informs you that a bell will ring thirty minutes before the incoming tide will cover the causeway and that when you hear it you must leave or wait the several hours until low tide. Pointing to a path which leads to the right of the chapel she tells you that this will take you back to the causeway when you are ready to leave. She smiles, bows slightly and departs.

Crossing the grass you approach the small chapel, a building no more than thirty feet in length and fifteen feet wide. The roof is unusual in that it appears to be a continuation of the walls joining at the apex in a small arch. There is a small doorway to the rear of the building, you open the heavy wooden door and step inside. Three steps go downward into the chapel and you step carefully down in the low light. The walls are whitewashed and here and there are faint outlines of painted scenes that you cannot quite distinguish.

You catch your breath with wonder as you take in the scene as your eyes become accustomed after the bright light outside. To the East there is an Altar covered in a sea blue cloth with beautiful embroidery in silver thread depicting many mystical symbols. Upon the Altar are two large candles and hanging from the ceiling is an intricately wrought holder containing a glass globe in which burns the sacred flame with a strange blue light.

But most beautiful of all is the window above the Altar. The design is that of an eight-pointed star with the top and bottom points elongated, the light shines through in ever changing patterns of light and colour as if a thousand diamonds gave it life. The longer you watch the more intense becomes the light until your whole vision is filled with its wonder.

There are several chairs which are designed to be comfortable for long periods of meditation in the chapel and before the Altar are several kneeling pads. You sit in one of the chairs and allow yourself to become absorbed in the Light streaming through the window and it takes your thoughts deep into meditation and fills you with the profoundest thoughts of exalted love and wisdom.

(*pause for music*)

It seems you sit for a long time until the sound of a bell brings you back to an awareness of your surroundings and you realise the tide must be rising and it is time to leave.

Rising you make your salutation to the Light and with a last lingering glance reluctantly leave the Chapel, knowing you may return and any time you wish, and go out into the sunlight closing the door softly behind you. Following the path the girl indicated, you walk across the grass and follow it round the castle walls, then going through a short passageway you find yourself back in the outer courtyard and passing through the archway you see the beginning of the causeway.

There is no time to linger as the sea is already beginning to wash over the edge of the pathway. Moving swiftly you hurry along the causeway looking down once more into the clear water. You walk steadily for some time watching the shore rapidly come nearer. Once more you are on the beach and the dry sand sinks about your feet as you step off the pathway. Walking slowly towards the sand hills the scene begins to become cloudy and you find yourself once more in the light mist which swirls gently about you. Gradually it clears and you can hear the small sounds about you and the familiar feel of your body sitting here in the room. Move and open your eyes and return to full wakefulness.

The Tree

You are standing in a wild wood; the trees crowd close about you and the atmosphere is heavy with the smell of autumn. Beneath your feet is a golden carpet of newly fallen leaves and the bright sunlight shines on the silver cobwebs glistening with morning dew. In front of you is a narrow path, you follow your impulse to see where it leads to and set off walking through the wood.

 It is quite beautiful here, the silence is almost tangible besides the bird song and the small sounds of little animals moving through the undergrowth.

 After walking for a short time the path opens out into a large grassy clearing. In the centre of the clearing is a large solitary tree. You cannot decide what variety it is as the leaves do not seem familiar. Some of its massive branches bend to touch the earth, forming small cave like areas where the leaves have not yet fallen, while its tallest branches reach high into the sky. It is a quite magnificent tree and it is almost if the wood does not dare encroach near to it out of respect.

With irresistible attraction you are drawn towards the Tree. As you come near it is like walking into a canopy of peace, the atmosphere of the Tree seems to enfold you and draw you in. Indeed, that is just what happens, for without seeming to encounter any resistance you find yourself INSIDE the trunk. It is like being in a warm and comfortable small room with rough barklike walls. It does not feel in any way threatening, on the contrary you feel safe, secure and protected.

Looking upwards you can see right to the top of the trunk and the massive branches forming criss-cross patterns against the blue sky. The sun creeps across to shine directly above you, a great golden flood of light dazzles your eyes and floods downwards through the trunk. It bathes you in its warm splendour as it passes and you tingle with its power as it goes through the top of your head, down and out through the soles of your feet. In your mind you follow its flow and see it go down into the spreading roots of the Tree, watch it nourish the soil and give vitality to every growing thing for yards around. Indeed, the whole wood feeds on it.

The Tree has stood in this place for hundreds of years and seems content that this should be so, it seems to laugh softly at you for thinking that your mobility is such a highly prized gift! Feel the stability of the Tree, marvel at the enormous root system spreading out below ground for many yards in all directions, and the tiny rootlets which gather nourishment and play their vital part in the sustenance of this great Tree.

Far below in the depths of the Earth you feel an answering response and the energies of Earth flow upwards, returning the vitality of the Light to its source, transformed into the energies of Life. The power flows into you as well, strengthening and empowering your physical being. A great pulse starts to beat in the region of your solar plexus and you recognise the rhythm of the life force within you, which sustains and maintains your physical body.

Almost with a sense of an explosion the down-pouring Light and the rising power meet in the region of your heart centre. The sensation creates an expansion of emotion within you and a great love, for this unique world of which you are a part, floods your being. You know your kinship both with the Light above and the Power below. Allow yourself to experience this feeling and let it flow outwards from your heart centre.

You feel identified with the Tree as if you and it have one existence, you know it's needs and understand its being. You bend with the wind as it sings in its branches and dance with the quivering leaves.

You become aware that the clearing is no longer empty. Six figures are emerging from the surrounding forest and converging about the Tree.

Journeys in the Light Within

The first figure you notice is a tall and graceful woman, her long trailing gown is black as the night sky and star spangled so that it glitters and shines as she moves. She is neither old nor young and yet has the beauty of youth and the dignity and authority of age. In her hands she bears a silver chalice from which sparkling water splashes as she walks. From the opposite side of the glade a man walks towards her. He wears a heavy ceremonial robe in the colour of grey storm clouds, the hood of his robe obscures his face but you can just see his thick grey beard which belies the virile power of his bearing. This man is in the full strength of his manhood yet venerable with years of experience. In his right hand he carries an ornate staff of office and you know it is no mere symbol but a magical instrument of great power.

As you watch you see another couple step into the clearing, one from the east and one from the west. From the East comes a regal figure, his robes of deep, almost violet, blue, are encrusted with jewels and rich embroidery in intricate heraldic designs. Upon his head is a royal crown and in his hand he carries a golden orb surmounted by the cross of sovereignty. The woman coming to meet him wears a scarlet gown, about its hem are embroidered green and golden leaves in all the different hues of the changing seasons. In her hand she carries a mighty sword, its bare and shining blade held upright, pointing to the skies.

The last two of the six figures come to complete the company. You catch your breath at the beauty of the woman who floats across the grass, clad in the flimsiest of gossamer green gowns, her golden hair floating behind her in the breeze, she holds a single blood red rose at the peak perfection of its bloom. Her companion who comes to meet her is a young man of golden hair and fresh un-bearded face whose orange robe flows about him with an almost feminine grace. In his right hand he carries a perfect cubic stone, cut and polished to perfection.

The six figures converge about the Tree and you know it is for you that they are there. As if the Tree trunk were no more solid than the air they circle about you. Then into your hand is placed the cubic stone, upon your breast is fastened the perfect rose, and into your other hand is placed the Orb. Then the mighty sword is lifted high and brought down, flat bladed, upon your head and you feel yourself forever changed and charged with its power. The staff of office touches you upon both shoulders and you feel the weight of its responsibility. Finally the Lady offers you the cup and brings it close so that you might drink. You touch your lips to the brim and sip the sparking water, it flows through you like fire and your consciousness shoots upwards to become one with the great Light which shines above the Tree.

It seems a long time before you become once more aware of your surroundings and you find yourself standing, alone once more, in the clearing beside the great Tree. You touch it's bark in salutation and gratitude, then turn and walk back towards the path you entered by. With one last backward glance at the Tree, you enter the wood and walk the path which brings you back into your own time and place in this room.

The Inner Temple

You begin your meditation within this Temple, your own particular sacred space. For a time allow your body to rest here in comfort so that your inner consciousness may be free to go deeply into another reality and for a time dwell within an Inner Temple which can be especially your own. This place is not just for to-day, in this meditation, but is somewhere you can build as a place of retreat and sanctuary which you may visit any time to refresh your inner self and gain strength for your work in the world.

You are walking across a lush green meadow, the sun is warm and the grass beneath your feet is full of bright flowers, humming bees and sparks where the sun reflects from the shining dew.

In the distance you see a hill rising from the meadow and on its summit stands a magnificent building. It is built of the whitest marble and gleams in the sunshine so brightly that you cannot discern the details of its structure.

Soon you reach the far side of the meadow and see a pathway winding up the hillside, you follow it and begin to climb. The rise is gentle and pleasant and you are surprised how easily you ascend. In a short time you have reached the top of the hill and the building stands before you.

It is a huge structure and you can see there are many great windows and the exterior is decorated with many beautiful carvings. It is like a great Cathedral and yet there are subtle differences in design and structure.

Before you is the great doorway, cast in bronze. On each door is set the figure of a great Archangel, each with its hand extended towards the visitor in greeting and with its great wings stretched on either side as if to enfold you in their protection.

You slowly pass through the doorway into the entrance porch and the sound of music draws you within. Follow the music and go inside.

In the centre of the Temple there is a beautiful circular Altar on which burns a single living flame. There are carved wooden seats surrounding the large clear space about the Altar, some are already occupied and you are invited to take your place, doing so you allow the peace and tranquillity to fill your being.

(*pause*)

Journeys in the Light Within

You rise and continue your exploration. At the far end of the Temple there is a flight of curving stone steps leading downwards, you descend them and find yourself in another Temple. This place is solidly built for it carries the weight of the building above, yet its arches and pillars are beautiful in their functional structure. It is obvious that a ceremony is about to start as two young people are quietly lighting candles and making preparations.

A procession of robed men walks into view and you decide to stay and join in their ceremony.

(*pause*)

The ceremony concludes and as the choir leaves in procession you decide to continue your exploration of the Temple. On the far side of the crypt is another flight of stairs similar to those you entered by, you climb them and find yourself once more in the main Temple. All is quiet and only the flame on the Altar moves.

You notice a small archway carved with delicate tracery and beyond it an almost transparent blue drapery which moves and shimmers as if in a slight breeze. There is a great feeling of unspoken invitation about the archway and you approach it and pass through. Within is a circular chamber, lit by tall windows of deepest blue with star patterns engraved in silver upon them. The effect is to fill the chamber with a rich blue light as of a moonlit evening. The black marble floor is decorated only by a large inlaid silver star – the chamber is otherwise empty except for a small raised platform opposite the entrance. As you watch a glow of light begins to shine about the platform and before you the figures of two women in dark blue robes form. One carries a single candle in an ornate holder, the other carries a cup of gold, unadorned yet unbelievably beautiful in its shape and radiance.

The woman holding the cup steps forward to the front of the small platform and holding it out towards you, bids you drink of the golden water of life it contains. You do so and feel renewed vitality and blessing flow though you.

Slowly the vision of the women fades and you turn and leave the chamber.

You make your way back into the main Temple taking with you the Blessing of the Sanctuary and knowing you may return whenever you have need.

You linger a little longer in the main Temple enjoying its beauty but knowing your visit is drawing to a close.

You have reached the main doorway and walk back out into the sunshine. Soon you are descending the path down the hill and you are back walking across the meadow and back into this room bringing with you a memory of your Inner Temple and what you experienced there. Come back and centre yourself once more into your physical body.

The Star

The Temple is quiet and still, allow any outside noises to drift across your mind and disappear.

Close your eyes and sink down slowly into relaxation, at the same time keeping your mind aware and awake.

Look into the darkness before you, it is deep and velvety black and you see no forms within it.

At your feet there is just the first faint feeling of seeing something – it is a pathway which is almost as dark as everything else around you. Gradually the darkness becomes less dense – and now you can now see the pathway and you begin to walk along it.

Ahead of you the sky lightens and the first hint of

the rising Moon glimmers on the horizon.

Against this ever-brightening sky you see two massive shapes, they are two immense pylons towering high above you and the path you are walking upon passes straight between them

A loud shout of HALT startles you and you stand still. You now notice that on either side of the path stands a tall and challenging figure, you had not noticed them before, in the shadows where they stand against the pylons.

You are questioned about your reasons for walking this path – you respond and eventually are allowed to pass. What did you tell them?

As you walk towards the pylons it appears as if the rising Moon is balanced between them. You continue and pass between these massive pillars, the Moon rises above your head and the landscape is flooded with its silver light.

Straight ahead you notice a small but very intense light shining in the sky, it looks like a distant star, but then as you watch it appears to move. It grows larger and brighter, it spins and increases in size, like a gigantic Catherine wheel spinning towards you through the night sky. It grows and grows until it fills your view, when suddenly it stops moving, shimmers and forms into a beautiful woman who holds out a hand to you in invitation.

What does she say to you and what does she show you?

(*pause for personal meditation*)

You find yourself once more standing on the pathway, watching a bright light gradually grow smaller until it is once more a pinpoint of light in the night sky.

You feel a small sadness at being once more alone but warmed by the memory of what you have learned. You turn and retrace your steps between the pylons and head once more into the darkness. You become aware of your physical body sitting in this room and you come back to full awareness of the Temple and open your eyes.

The Perennial Story
A Tarot Journey

History is the recorded version of events that have happened in the material objective world. What is recorded may or may not be accurate or truthful, however our culture presents you with a particular viewpoint of past events and our tendency is to accept this as unchallenged fact. It is a useful exercise to learn to question and cross check what we are told.

A myth is a traditional story that appeals to the consciousness of a people by embodying its cultural and spiritual ideals or by expressing commonly felt emotions. Myth describes and transmits in allegorical and symbolic form eternal truths through stories, which themselves are not necessarily factually true.

Journeys in the Light Within

These stories do however have a reality in our imagination and spiritual consciousness that gives them as much power and influence as any outer authority or event.

It is important to remember that all experience is an inner reality whether it is generated by external or internal events. No conscious experience is ever had in the outer material world, it is always known within the mind.

In our lives we ourselves have a history, we are born in a particular place, live and work with people and circumstances around you and eventually we die. Yet we live our lives in the midst of myth. We are physical humans living in a practical scientific world, yet we are also sparks of consciousness whose realm is within.

Our particular society, culture and race also have a history and a story. We learn these from our earliest years and often there is no clear distinction between objective truth and subjective myth. The two become confused and the story is presented as fact and fact as myth (or the creation of imagination.)

The story of our physical material life is like one snake winding around the caduceus, the other snake is the story of our spiritual self, that spark of the Divine which exists within each one of us. The winged rod around which the snakes twine is the realm of the Divine in which we live and move and have our being. It is the symbol of Divinity manifesting as matter and Divinity manifesting as the immaterial spiritual inner realms.

We are children of that Divinity, issuing forth from the Creative Centre to incarnate in the material world so that we may learn and grow.

THE FOOL
We are The Fool

We come naked of spirit, taking on the garment of mortality, bringing with you little other than a fading memory of our origin and true nature. We are urged on by raw nature jumping at our heels, we too must become a part of the world of nature for in our bodies we are bound to her rules and necessities. It is a leap into the unknown, a one-way journey, it is the beginning of life.

Each one of us has made this so called 'fall' into materiality. So too have the heroes and saviour gods of our stories who have descended into incarnation in myth to become personalities in our imagination.

THE MAGICIAN
The Magician is a part of our goal, he represents the one who has achieved what we are aiming to achieve. He has learnt to be master of the Elements of Earth, Air, Fire and Water. He does not work magic in the sense of circumventing the natural laws of the manifest world, rather does he learn their functions and use their natural forces to accomplish results in accordance with his will. He lives in harmony with nature and wields controlled power over his world. He works through knowledge, investigation, experiment and results. He is the wizard, shaman or alchemist hero of our stories who commands all nature to his will. He is ourselves when we have accomplished our tasks.

THE PRIESTESS

The Priestess is the inner consciousness and spirit, which is in the body but is untouched by the flesh. She is ever virgin for she does not partake of the needs of worldly life. She is the still voice within for she carries wisdom and teaching in her hand.

The Priestess is the Virgin Mother of all saviour gods and solar heroes because they too are not of the flesh, they live only in their stories, they are vehicles by and through whom the Priestess transmits her wisdom to the children of Earth.

THE EMPRESS

The Empress is very much in the material world. She is all nature, its natural environment, its plants and animals. She is fecundity and fertility; she nurtures the seed of life and brings it to maturity and birth. She is the eternal Mother, we partake of her nature, for our bodies are born of her flesh. The Empress rules over all feminine aspects of the polarities of material creation, she is Binah of the Tree of Life.

In myth the Empress is the Goddess of all our stories, she abides in the heavens and is crowned with stars, the Moon is beneath her feet and she is ever pregnant with the powers of manifestation. She is too the archetypal mother to the saviour gods, it is she who nurtures them to maturity, surrenders them to their mission and grieves at their eventual sacrifice.

THE EMPEROR

The Emperor is the lover and partner of the Empress, he is the Father of her progeny, the generator of all life. In the material world he rules over system and order in physical life. He is that aspect of our body and mental self, which makes possible the organisation of civilisation.

He lives in our minds and hearts as the legendary King Arthur, the Once and Future King, and Solomon the Wise, and other perfect rulers who wait beneath the allegorical mountain and who will one day rise to free the nations. He is masculine power in men and strength and endurance in woman. In the spiritual realms he is the Father god who religion sees as watching over you, defending and judging us.

THE HIEROPHANT
The Hierophant or Pope has two aspects. As Hierophant he is the one who teaches and expounds upon the sacred mysteries, he is an interpreter of esoteric and arcane knowledge. In our personal story he is the Teacher who lifts the veil of the Mystery for us, who helps us to begin to discover our true nature and to understand that to believe is not a virtue, for belief does not bestow truth or integrity on what is believed. The Mysteries ever taught and teach that only of our own knowledge and experience shall we know Truth. And when we too in our turn have learnt, then must we too become the Hierophant, for we cannot always remain the taught and must become the teacher.

Yet the Hierophant is also a figure of power and authority and these can be abused and become harmful both in the material and spiritual worlds. He can, by the use of worldly power, impose his will upon both our bodies and minds, he can be rigid orthodoxy to a particular belief, bigotry in our viewpoints and an inner image to which we surrender our own will and mind. We have the potential to become the Hierophant but we have too the potential to surrender our freedom to him.

THE LOVERS

Of all the characters in our lives and stories, perhaps the most potent are The Lovers. Love has many meanings in our lives, it is the love and protection of our parents, it is caring for each other, it is feeling responsible for our Earth and all its creatures, it is the love we feel towards Divinity. It is that need we feel for a partner to share our journey, a parent for our children and a companion on our spiritual quest.

To choose the best partner is not always easy, we can be dazzled by glamour and beauty and not see the incompatibility inherent in our mutual characters. We can be lured into relationships by consideration of wealth and position, not seeing how empty such relationships can become. The path of the Lovers is about choice, it is also about clear sight and understanding of ourselves and others. Love is perhaps our greatest Teacher because for its sake we will undergo experiences that nothing else would persuade us to go through.

Our myths are full of great love stories, each of which can tell us something of the good and the bad of relationships. Many of our modern-day myths can miss-lead because we believe that the perfect partners of story can exist for us in material life, forgetting that such perfection is often but a projection of our own wish fulfilment. To receive love we must give love, indeed the ideal of the Mysteries is unconditional love, when we love because we love and without seeking to receive.

THE CHARIOT
Each of us is the ruler of The Chariot of our bodies, it is ours to direct and use. We decide its course between the polarities of choice, we can do good or evil, act with wisdom or foolishness, conserve our wealth or spend into poverty, be aggressive or peaceful, create beauty or ugliness in our lives, we can love or we can hate, we can even decide whether we live or we die. In myth the chariot is our spiritual consciousness, that body of light in which we can enter the hidden worlds of the spirit and journey to inner realms, it is consciousness on all its many levels.

JUSTICE
The Universe in which we live operates in accordance with Law and Justice. Some of the laws we have discovered and can use to our advantage, others remain unknown and their effects appear mysterious and arbitrary. For every cause there is an effect, for every action a reaction. This balance of the scales we call Justice. In our material world humans do not always get things right and in the short-term justice is not always the outcome of our legal processes. But in the totality of the inner and outer worlds and in the fullness of time Justice always prevails. The right effect will follow the cause. This is what we call Karma. All belief systems have some form of judgement that follows physical death and this is believed to be dispensed with absolute Justice. For some it is their God who judges, for some it is Anubis

weighing the heart against the Feather of Maat and for some it is The Devil claiming his own. Whatever the reality may be behind the myths we can be assured it will be in accordance with immutable Law.

So whatever our particular way of looking at our lives and the reasons for our existence, we are all in the process of learning. Whatever experiences we go thorough, it is impossible to do so without learning something, even if only the very undesirable effects of some of our actions. It is said that experience is the great Teacher, but we are not left alone to struggle with our lessons without either human or spiritual teachers to assist us.

THE HERMIT

The Hermit represents our material plane Teachers, those great souls who appear from time to time in human history and illumine our species with their wisdom and insights. They hold up a lamp that shines down the centuries in books and teachings and we are indeed blessed if we have the privilege of meeting such a one in our lives. Then there are those who teach from the inner realms, they speak to us in the quiet of our mind, theirs are the voices of intuition and inspiration, the insights of meditation and the teachings we receive in dreams. The voices of Teachers such as Mithras and Jesus, the Buddha and Mohammed, Thoth and Anubis, and Merlin and the Wise Women speak to us through their stories, they teach through their myths and they live in our inner worlds where we may meet them if we will.

WHEEL OF FORTUNE

The drama of our lives is played out on the stage of Earth, ever moving within the cycles of nature, of winter and summer, autumn and spring, of the vast cycles of the Sun and of the stars. All nature turns and comes back again to its beginnings, its elemental powers ever empowering or destroying its children.

The great Wheel of Life ever turns taking us with it on its endless spinning. Sometimes our fortunes are climbing on the rim of happiness and success, only to reach the height of the circle and turn downwards towards failure and despair. These changes may not be extreme in our lives but they always occur to some degree, never believe you have reached the pinnacle of attainment either in your material life or your spiritual for the wheel must turn as night follows day and day follows night.

STRENGTH

Behind everything, material and spiritual, is energy. The nature of our manifest world, as we see it, is an illusion, it is in fact vibrating energy.

Within the nature of the most solid object, at its smallest atomic structure we find only space and vibration. This energy is eternal and indestructible; through its various wavelengths and frequencies the stars of the heavens and the manifestations of earth are formed. We ourselves are made of this FORCE. It controls, designs and IS everything. Material manifestation is animated by it, the strongest animal, the largest building, the most intelligent human, cannot exist without it, We and all nature are helpless in its hands, we submit because we must to its control and rule; for we are this energy manifesting.

HANGED MAN

In our stories the image of the Hanged Man has more than one meaning. It is the body vehicle in which the eternal spirit is temporarily encased caught in the material world and subject to its trials, tribulations, joys and achievements. We call this process incarnation. Looked at from the reverse direction the man appears relaxed and almost dancing as he descends. We do not come into life against our will however much we struggle with its experiences once we are here.

In myth this character represents the dying saviour gods and solar deities who sacrifice their place in the Divine worlds in order to demonstrate eternal truths in the mythological realms, they are born in their stories, teach in their mission, and are killed or otherwise sacrificed for the sake of humanity and then rise again to prove the immortality of the soul. We hear their story told over and over again, it is the story of Tammuz, Adonis, Atys, Osiris, Jesus, Odin and many more. It symbolises the human spirit suspended from heaven by a single thread, never losing its contact with the Divine. Wisdom not death is the reward for this voluntary sacrifice. As the human soul is suspended above the world of illusion and unreality it is rewarded by the attainment of self-realisation.

DEATH

Apart from our birth the one experience none of us can escape is our own bodies Death. No matter our status in life, be we king or pauper, noble or peasant, adult or child, each of us must in time surrender our body back to the earth, return our life back into the vast reservoir from which it sprang. In our lives we encounter many little deaths, our endeavours fail, we meet undesirable and difficult changes, our loved ones leave us, yet such changes are the eternal flow of life and prepare us for the greatest change of all. Death of the body is the great liberator for it frees us from pain and suffering both of the body and of memory of the cost of each phase of our learning. The sacrificed saviours teach us their message that death is but an event and that we too in our essential immortal spirit will rise again when we are freed from the bondage of physical existence.

TEMPERANCE
Our eternal soul, once free of the material world, 'ascends' into the spiritual immaterial realms. Yet we do not remain there, time after time we come back to Earth to continue our evolution, the Waters of Life and Spirit are constantly poured from one vessel into another. The body form changes, the circumstances of our lives are different, but life and soul continue. Embarking on each journey we bring with us a little more in our 'bag of the Fool' in the form of intuitive knowledge, the wisdom gained from our past experiences and a store of memory which we may not be able to access at will but which from time to time awakens in our consciousness.

This is the lesson that the Sacrificed Gods teach in their stories, Osiris was re-membered and rose again from death to become God of the Underworld,

Tammaz died at mid-summer to be resurrected with great rejoicing. Adonis was gored to death by a wild boar and after three days, or sometimes months, rose triumphant on 25th March. Atys again died after being gored by a wild boar, or in some accounts by a wound inflicted under a pine tree and, after remaining three days in the tomb rose again upon a date corresponding with Easter morn And by this resurrection overcame death for all who were initiated into his mysteries. Jesus was born on the 25th December, slain at Easter and in three days rose again and ascended into heaven. All these events and their dates correspond with the seasons of the year, important dates in the cycles of the Sun and of Earth. The dying/sacrificed gods teach in their myths the eternal cyclic nature of life on Earth and in their resurrection they teach that we too rise from our bodily death into our spiritual body of light, and continue.

THE DEVIL
Life on Earth offers many kinds of experience, if we learn the lesson of each we grow in our spiritual self. But we too can become trapped in the material life of Earth. We can seek wealth and power to the exclusion of all else, become blind to the consequences of our actions, fail to listen to the voice of our inner consciousness. The thrill of battle and conflict can become addictive and all compassion leave us as we slaughter and torture for selfish ends. We can enslave our bodies to the gratification of our body appetites, allowing the desire for food and sensuality or the illusions of alcohol and drugs to take over control of

our body vehicle. We place these chains about ourselves, yet we are free to remove them at any time we so choose. In myth we see the Devil as the one who inflicts these evils upon us, tempts us into disaster, leads us astray, but he is only the witness of our own self-inflicted torture.

THE TOWER

Striving to achieve is a part of Earth life, we all want to make our surroundings as comfortable as possible. Artists wish to beautify our world, actors to entertain and educate us, teachers to improve our minds. Monetary systems encourage us to accumulate wealth so we may provide more luxuries to our way of life. Fame and fortune are seductive sirens!

Yet however high we climb, no matter how famous we may become none of us are immune to the possibility of losing everything. Disaster can strike at any time and we find ourselves thrown back on our basic resources. Disasters can be manmade or a part of the natural world. Earthquakes shake the earth, storm and floods wreak havoc, diseases break out, all these things can bring our world crashing down around us.

The material world is ever unstable and changeable, only our inner consciousness is constant and dependable.

The Sacrificed Gods in their stories all have their times of triumph, their hour of acclaim and success but always they lose, or surrender, everything of earth in their final sacrifice.

THE STAR

In our hearts and minds Humanity has always thought of the heavens as the realm of the gods and of spiritual existence. The stars shining against the blackness of the night sky seem to radiate influence into our lives. From time immemorial they have been thought to influence our very characters and life patterns. They are indeed the way-showers of our travels and indicators of our seasons.

Yet it is in the depths of the inner realms, which lie within and behind material manifestation, that we find the true source of our intuitions and wisdom. Our consciousness is part of that vast spiritual reservoir and with each lifetime, from what we learn, a little more is poured back into it as we meld once more into our Source. The Way-showers and Teachers are sparks of Divine Light and Wisdom, radiant stars shining in the darkness of our ignorance. Be they physical humans or mythological characters makes no difference, they shine and if we are wise we follow where they lead.

Among our Shining Stars are Moses the Lawgiver, Buddha the Compassionate, Confucius the Teacher of Justice, Zoroaster the Priest of the Sun, Plato the Wise One, Jesus the Teacher of Righteousness, Origen the Truth Seeker and Mohammed the Prophet.

THE MOON

So important are our hours of consciousness that we tend to forget that a large portion of our lives is spent in sleep. This necessary time of restoration of our physical bodies is not a time of inactivity in our spiritual lives. For when sleep comes, so too do our dreams; those enigmatic inner scenarios we nightly live through. From the earliest of times dreams have been regarded as a part of our spiritual life. So important indeed that in pre-Christian times Temples were dedicated to inducing them and interpreting their images and stories. Dreams seem to happen in a space/time where the rules of the waking world do not apply. Many are the reports of pre-cognitive and prophetic dreams that have come to pass. Of people met in dreams who come into our waking lives, of problems solved and inventions made as a result of the solutions dreams present. Dreams arise from those levels of the mind which lie deeply beyond our waking access, it is the same inner world from which spring our mystical insights and experiences. We have within us a treasure house of images from which our waking and dream stories arise to instruct and enlighten us. This realm of dream has always been considered to be under the influence of the Moon. From ancient times it has been regarded as representative of the feminine and of water which ebbs and flows under its influence. It is the great symbol of the sub-conscious mind, It is a symbol too of Isis the archetypal feminine Goddess. Its stories have to do with mystery and hidden worlds, of illumination in the darkest night both in the natural world and in the dark night of the soul. The Moon has the power to, from time to time, eclipse the Sun, turning day into night. So too the powers the Moon represents can obscure and overshadow our waking lives. Her domain is a world of things half seen, of recurring cycles and hidden wisdom.

THE SUN

As the Moon rules the night, so does the Sun rule the day. Each dawn its bright splendour floods our world with light. Its warmth gives life and vitality to all living things. Small wonder that it has been worshipped since the beginning of time in differing guises and under many names. In Egypt the Sun was personified as the gods Ra and Horus, in Greece as Helios and Apollo, in Celtic lands as Lugh, in Rome as Mithras, in Christianity as Jesus Son of the Sun, indeed in all cultures there has always been a solar God, the Sol Invictus, the unconquerable Sun.

The Sun rules every moment of our lives, we draw our life from it, our bodies are atoms of its fiery structure.

As our lives are the Sun in manifestation so too are the solar heroes and the events of their lives reflections of the risings and settings, cycles and seasons created by the Sun, they are born at mid-winter, are slain and resurrected at the vernal equinox, triumph at the summer solstice and sometimes die at the winter solstice to be re-born or resurrected three days later when the sun once more begins its return.

JUDGEMENT

In all the stories the saviour character represents the Divine Principle which incarnates, dies and rises again on behalf of all humanity. And it is too the story of each one of us who is born, lives and dies, yet rises again and again in our journey towards spiritual life and perfection.

The tomb is the resting place of the body but the

realms of Light are the home and the destination of that immortal Divine Spark which dwells within each one of us.

THE WORLD
Free of the ties of mortal life the soul rejoices in its victory. It dwells with the mighty spiritual powers and garners the fruits of its recent incarnation. It has returned home and knows the ineffable Light and Glory of the Inner Realms.

THE FOOL
And then we set out once more upon another journey!

The Rhythms of Force and Form

The manifest world within which we live consists of energy or force and the forms into which this energy organises itself, thus appearing to us as physical reality. The tools we use to record and describe energy in action are what we generally term symbols, these are a kind of shorthand used to describe ideas in a concise way and to communicate ideas and meanings for which language is often inadequate. They range from the basic tools of everyday life such as numbers and alphabet to the complicated and profound conveying of deep spiritual truths.

Energy underlies everything. We can study how energy works by the conventional scientific means available in our modern world. But there are some levels of energy which science has not yet learned to measure but which we as students of the more subtle energies can demonstrate and use.

Numbers are used to express the complexities of natural law and those principles that underlie the structure and functioning of the natural world. Each of the first ten numbers has a profound meaning, each demonstrates an eternal law which is universal within creation. By learning the science of numbers we learn the structure of manifestation and the concepts of Infinity and Unity.

This use of numbers as symbols generally deals with the first ten numbers. It is not mathematics, which is the applied use of numbers in a specific manner. The use of numbers as symbols goes back to the ancient roots of philosophy and spiritual studies. So to look at the meanings attributed to numbers.

Everything starts with a point, the one, the Unity from which all originates. When it is joined to a second point they becomes a line and a line extended in a particular direction becomes a circle. A circle cannot exist without a line, as a line without a point cannot exist. The point and the monad, or one, must be the beginning for all things and symbols. Whatever exists at the periphery of anything must have a relationship with the centre point from which everything begins

So we have one and two; then three represents a triangle, the ternary.

The square represents four or the quaternary. Five

represents a pentagon, six a hexagon, seven a heptagon and eight the octagon, nine the nonagon and ten the decagon.

The ancient esoteric meanings of the numbers were;

1. The One is unchangeable, has no parts, is multiplied by itself and its product is also the one. It is the beginning and the end of all numbers. Yet it itself has no beginning or end. It is the symbol of itself, a symbol of unity and accord.
2. The number 2 is the first number as it is the first multitude. Its measure is the 1 from which it comes. It is the symbol of production, creation, the number of knowledge, love and union.
3. The number 3 is the first independent number and is called "holy". It is the symbol of perfection and the first cubical figure.
4. The number 4 is the number of bodies, a symbol of solidity, and the things of the corporal world are measured by it.
5. The number 5 is the appearance of the first odd number combined with the first even number (3+2). It is a symbol of justice and union.
6. The number 6 is a seal of peace, a symbol of perfection and contentment. It is also called the human number and the number of work and service.
7. The number 7 is the number of human life. It is called the number of birth, education and being, and is a symbol of cognition, repentance and forgiveness as well as a symbol of time.
8. Is the number of fulfilment and justice, a symbol of the destruction of transitory things,

the number of bliss and joy.
9. Is the number of All-Wisdom and knowledge, a symbol of man's sciences.
10. Is the universe, the number of the entire human life and the number of law.
11. Has no significance.
12. Is the number of perfection and grace.

Such was the main definition of numbers by the ancients.

These numbers and the shapes that represent them are highly symbolic.

One is the number of Divinity, the Creator.

Two is polarity, the first separation into positive and negative, male and female.

Three represent the three aspects of Being, the body, spirit and soul of humanity, also the trinity of, two causes and their result, which is the pattern underlying all Creation.

The quaternary is often the four Elements of Air, Fire, Water and Earth that the Alchemists saw as the four principles of creation.

The quaternary is represented by two lines crossing, thus forming the four lines of a cross. It is also a square representing foundation and completion.

The five-sided pentagon represents the form of humanity.

The six-sided hexagram the interlacing of the above and the below.

The seven-sided heptagon the seven ancient planets, seven days of the week and many other sevens in esoteric work.

Journeys in the Light Within

The eight-sided octagon has been called the chaos star and Venus star, it was also used to represent many of the other ancient gods and goddesses.

Nine and ten are used in symbolic imagery but the meanings attached are more generalised.

Solid Figures

The properties of solid figures have kept mathematicians occupied for centuries. Sometimes called polyhedrons, these are formed from regular polygons, such as squares and triangles, and, despite their best efforts, mathematicians have so far failed to find any more than five of them. These five solid figures have been known since ancient Greek times, which is why they are sometimes referred to as the platonic solids. The five regular polyhedra are the tetrahedron (four triangular faces, the cube (six square faces), the octahedron (eight triangular faces), the dodecahedron (12 pentagonal faces and the icosahedron (20 triangular faces).

Sphere

The sphere can be thought of as a circle in three dimensions. Every point on the surface of a sphere lies at the same distance from its centre. As with a circle, this distance is known as the radius. Also just like a circle, a sphere has a circumference and a diameter. Slicing through the diameter of a sphere creates two equal hemispheres, the flat surfaces of which form circles.

Pyramids

The classic Egyptian style pyramid has triangular

sides, but unlike the tetrahedron it has a square base.

Dowsing
We can use the technique of dowsing to demonstrate some of the effects these numbers, shapes and diagrams manifest.

I would define three rules of dowsing.
1. The pendulum moves in response to MIND which knows at a level not accessible to consciousness.
2. Knowledge which exists within the Universal Mind is available to the conscious mind of humans by use of the pendulum.
3. The pendulum will respond to our thought, it will access the point of our focus whether this be where we look, where we point, or where we just focus our concentration.

Each person's response is different so we have to determine our own negative, positive and neutral responses.

My explanation of dowsing is that we use the principal of the mind causing the effects and that the pendulum is a mirror of our subconscious mind which in its turn has access to the Universal Mind. We, by our will, focus and direct the pendulum to respond to the natural vibrations such as the magnetic field of the earth, the vibrations caused by the movement of underground water, the life force of people and the atomic vibrations which all things by their mere existence possess.

Our sub-conscious mind becomes tuned into whatever we direct it to and a harmonic condition is created between the object, our mind, and the pendulum. Therefore since as we know from the teachings of the mystics, time and space do not exist in the realm of mind, distance and time are not involved, and the dowser can work as effectively over vast distances as they can when the thing they are seeking is near at hand..

The ability to use the pendulum and to be an accurate and effective dowser has been thought to be a gift bestowed on certain individuals. But in fact this is not so, everyone has the ability, it is part of the abilities of the human mind - some people inhibit their ability by their own disbelief and others develop it by practice; but it is latent in us all.

It is also important that we have a need to know the answers we are seeking; inaccurate results very often occur when we are only seeking to show that dowsing works. Thus we must avoid several things;

1. doubt.
2. using the brain instead of MIND
3. wishful thinking
4. anticipating the answers and
5. having preconceived. ideas of what the answers will be.
6. getting overconfident
7. allowing the discipline of the mind to slip.

Each symbolic shape has a vibration pattern specific to it. They have effects upon the observer and their environment.

The shape and direction of buildings are not accidental, they are so in order to manifest a specific condition in the physical world.

In the same way any symbolic pattern impressed

upon the landscape will have an effect.

Dowsing is a means of determining the vibratory pattern of shapes and symbols and aligning them to give their most beneficial effect by deliberately focussing their force and form.

A Dream

At the start of the dream I was standing with a group of about five others of like mind, we were talking about visiting another dimension. The entry to this dimension was before us, not as a specific wall but an area in space which I knew was the limit of the other world and the entry to it.

We walked through this boundary and everything was immediately different. There was no form to where we were in any earthly sense. There were buildings to our left, they had a kind of shape but this was more implied than actual. Rather than form I saw the molecules and atoms which composed the scene, they vibrated and shimmered in patterns which none the less conveyed the 'feeling' of buildings. There was a low continuous humming sound which the scene emitted.

We walked down a pathway and came to the edge of a cliff, before and below us spread a beautiful valley, the view spreading away into the distance.

I had in my hand a large sword which I raised high about my head and brought down before me plunging it into the ground at my feet. Immediately a ball of very intense light shot up the length of the sword, growing as it came. It rose into the sky in a vast column of brilliant, almost blinding, light. There were some clouds in the sky, the light went through a gap in the clouds then burst into an even more intense light and expanded in all directions. It was so bright I could see nothing else but this glowing column from earth to sky.

There is a gap in my memory after this although I know there was a great deal more.

Then I was walking up a rough lane with a companion, following us was a strange creature something like a large crab. This person turned and struck the creature, which immediately shattered into dozens of pieces, each of which was living and identical with the original creature, it was like breaking a hologram.

It seemed I spent quite some time in this place but cannot now recall the details. There was an intense sense of a different vibration, slightly menacing but very vibrant and 'alive' about the whole place, the feeling of this persisted after I awoke.

When I awoke there was a kind of silent click as everything switched back into the vibration of this

Universe.

I remember my first waking though was "That was simply amazing!"

THOUGHTS FOR MEDITATION

Manifestation is the state we are in as living beings in a physical universe.

The world around us, the earth, the stars, the heavens and the immensity of space, all are manifestations of the supreme energies of the Divine Creative Force.

We live in a physical body which is endowed with five senses of perception: sight, smell, touch, hearing and taste. These keep us informed about the world around us.

Internally we have the faculties of consciousness which keeps us informed about the world within us.

Consciousness is the mechanism of perception. Everything, of both internal and external origin, is registered and perceived by consciousness.

The human body is a very efficient vehicle and it is our responsibility to care for it so that we make its life as comfortable and trouble free as possible. So moderation is required in how we eat and drink, exercise and work our bodies.

The circumstances into which we are born, and the events of our lifetime, constitute the school in which we learn life's lessons.

Unfavourable circumstances and results which keep recurring indicate lessons we have not yet learned. They will keep recurring until we recognize the lesson and change how we deal with the problem.

It is important to recognize and understand the ethics and moral standards of the society in which we live.

To acquire knowledge is not necessarily to be wise, we must also gain understanding and experience to aspire to wisdom.

An immortal soul looks out from every human face, whatever its colour or race.

Every living creature has a level of consciousness, this may be different from the human but that is not to say it is less valid.

Every living creature experiences the same joy, needs, pains and fears.

Every living being takes what it needs from its environment. Human beings do not observe this law, they take what they want not what they need. Hence they deplete and damage their world to their own desolation.

Human consciousness is one aspect of Cosmic Consciousness.

The Universe is conscious and intelligent. It knows how to heal, how to modify living organisms to the needs of their environment and how to adjust the various systems of the planet for the best state of its health.

Intuition occurs when knowledge and wisdom rise to the surface of consciousness. It is when the mind touches the Greater Mind of the Cosmos.

Sleep is essential for the health of the body. Dreams are a function of sleep. At one level dreams are a clearing process of the mind and are often nonsensical and chaotic.
    At a deeper level they can be instructive and profound. At a very deep level we can become conscious in the dream and enter deeper levels of reality.

The plane of consciousness nearest to the physical is termed the astral plane. Perception on the astral plane is like a mirror image of the physical.

When consciousness is on the astral plane, we can

perceive the physical but as if it were a negative image.

When the mind is quiet it is possible to contact the Greater Mind of the cosmos. We can then request help in our difficulties. But this help must be for what we need, not for our wants.

To receive help from the Greater Mind we must ask, remember we were told "ask and ye shall receive." To help us without our asking would be to interfere with our free will.

However we imagine the Greater Mind, be it as a God, a Master or a Teacher, this is an image we create. What we receive is always in the form of a thought, sometimes so condensed it takes time to unravel the full meaning.

By our thoughts and actions, we can create an atmosphere of the sacred, the more people who join together in this the more powerful the result.

Learning to think for ourselves is one of the first steps in spiritual training.

To believe just because we are told to believe is not a virtue.

The aim of spiritual training is to learn to know from our own experience.

Each of us is an essential part of Creation, the universe would not be complete without us.

Our truth is always relative to our personal perspective.

Each of us is a spark of the Greater Light.

As we were told by a Great Master, "Seek and ye shall find, knock and it shall be opened unto you."

About the Author

Born in Colwyn Bay, North Wales, U.K. Elizabeth Anderton spent her early years in Wales and later in Cheshire.

By profession an Ophthalmic Optician, she is now retired from active practice.

Having an interest in spiritual and psychic matters from an early age, Elizabeth joined the Ancient Mystical Order Rosae Crucis in 1962 and followed their system of home study until 1990.

In 1979 she first made contact with local groups and soon became actively involved in the work of the Order serving as a Chapter and Grand Lodge Officer until her resignation in 1990.

From the beginning of the Order Militia Crucifera Evangelica in the United Kingdom in 1991, Elizabeth served as Marshal of the U.K.Priory until her appointment to the Sovereign Priory as Magister Templi of the Order in 1996. She retired from this Office in October 2009 having worked extensively with OMCE groups world-wide.

In 1981 she was Initiated into the Traditional Martinist Order serving as group member and as a 4th Degree Initiator.

In 1985 she was Initiated into Co-Masonic Free Masonry, Le Droit Humane, an International Order of Free Masonry open to both men and women..

Since becoming a student of the "Servants of the Light" School in 1982, Elizabeth worked extensively within the School and was a supervisor for the SOL course work from 1985 until her retirement in 2018.

During 1980 she met John A.B. Fox. From 1982 onwards they shared a working partnership of lectures and workshops which led to the eventual formation of their own "Sirius" title in 1990, under which they presented workshops and seminars both personally and organising them for many of the days fore-most Teachers. John and Elizabeth were married in 1992. After a short illness John died on 27 January 2002 which brought to a close their long partnership in esoteric work.

From 2002 until 2015 Elizabeth was co-presenter with Dolores Ashcroft-Nowicki, Director of Studies of SOL, in their series of thirteen annual Ritual with Purpose workshops.

Elizabeth now lives in Milford Haven, south west Wales, and has retired from group work. *Rituals of The Light Within* and now *Journeys in the Light Within* are now her contribution to The Work.

Recent Titles from Megalithica Books

Coming Forth by Day by Storm Constantine

This book explores the myths of Ancient Egyptian gods and goddesses – showing how their stories relate to aspects of our lives, hopes and aspirations, and how we can learn from these ancient narratives. Through 28 deep and evocative pathworkings and rituals, the author provides a rich and vivid system of magic that the practitioner – whether experienced or a novice – can utilize in the search for self-knowledge, and to help themselves, others and the world around them. ISBN: 978-1-912241-11-8 Price: £12.99, $16.99

SHE: Primal Meetings with the Dark Goddess by Storm Constantine & Andrew Collins

The Dark Goddess is unpredictable, dispassionate, cruel, and often deadly. She reflects our deepest desires, fears, hopes and expectations. In this fully-illustrated book, Storm Constantine and Andrew Collins have selected a fascinating range of 34 goddesses, including some who are not so well-known. The pathworkings to meet them and explore their realms will offer insight into these often-misunderstood deities. (This title is also available as a limited edition, numbered hardback.) ISBN: 978-1-912241-06-4 Price: £12.99, $18.99

My First Book of Magic by Dolores Ashcroft-Nowicki

I want to tell you how the Pagan Way works, what it does, and how it makes you feel. I want you to know the joy this oldest of all traditions can bring you. The way of sharing it with humans, elementals, sprites, animals, plants, trees, and of course other pagans.
If you have a child in your life that has the look of far memory in their eyes, gift them with this guide. If you remember the child you were, read this book and reopen the gates of your wonder." – Ivo Dominguez Jr., author of 'Keys to Perception'.
ISBN: 978-1-912241-10-1 Price: £10.99, $15.99

www.immanion-press.com

Egyptian Magic from Megalithica Books

Sekhem Heka by Storm Constantine

Drawing upon her experiences in Egyptian Magic and the energy healing systems of Reiki and Seichim, Storm Constantine developed this new system for practitioners of both magic and energy healing. Incorporating ritual and visualisation into a progressive journey through the seven energy centres of the body, Sekhem Heka can be practiced by those who are already attuned to an energy healing modality, as well as those who are simply interested in the magical aspects of the system. Sekhem Heka is designed to help the practitioner work upon self-evolution. Each of the seven tiers focuses upon a particular Ancient Egyptian god or goddess, including practical exercises and rites. ISBN pbk: 9781905713134, £12.99 $21.99

Graeco-Egyptian Magic by Tony Mierzwicki

This book outlines a daily practice involving planetary Hermeticism, drawn from the original texts and converted into a format that fits easily into the modern magician's practice. As a magickal system, Graeco-Egyptian magick represents the last flowering of paganism before it was wiped out by the Christian juggernaut. It is a hybrid system that blended ancient Sumerian and Egyptian magick with the relatively more modern Greek and Judaic systems. ISBN pbk: 9781912241033, £12.99 $21.99

The Travellers' Guide to the Duat by Kiya Nicoll

Planning a trip to the Egyptian spirit world? Like any responsible traveller, you want to know something about the history, geography, and politics of your destination. You want to know what documents you need to have in order for customs and immigration, what precautions to take, how to book a boat tour, where to stay, what to eat, and when you'll get the most interesting sightseeing opportunities. Laced through its humorous presentation you will find extensive information about ancient Egyptian religion and magical practice. Renditions of ancient spells in modern poetry mark each section, showing the ancient magical texts in a new light. The Beautiful West awaits! Book your tour today!
ISBN pbk: 9781905713738, $19.99, £10.99

www.immanion-press.com

www.ingramcontent.com/pod-product-compliance
Lightning Source LLC
LaVergne TN
LVHW041253080426
835510LV00009B/713